NEW WIRE CROCHET
Jewelry

interweave.com
penguinrandomhouse.com

1 3 5 7 9 10 8 6 4 2

ISBN 978 1 63250 693 1

Packaged by BlueRed Press Ltd. 2019
Designed by Insight Design Concepts Ltd.
Type set in Fairfield and Din Pro

NEW WIRE CROCHET
Jewelry

17 ELEGANT INVISIBLE SPOOL KNITTING DESIGNS

YAEL FALK

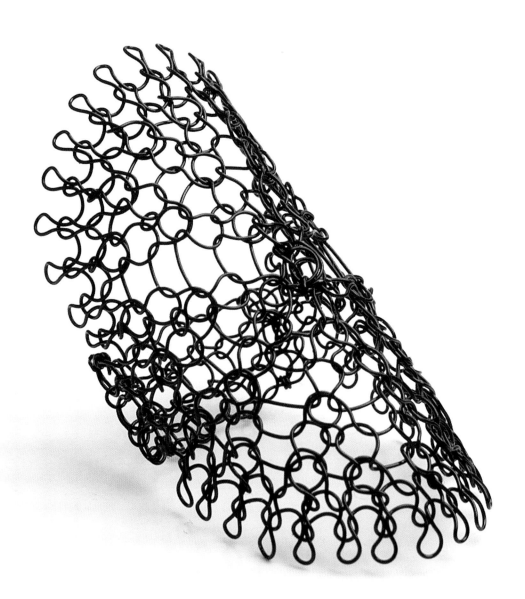

CONTENTS

MY STORY

My given name is Yael, but I'm known by friends and family as Yoola. I am an industrial designer by profession, but a metal crocheter and jewelry designer by heart and destiny.

Several years ago, when my husband's job relocated our young family to Switzerland, I became—for the first time in my life—a stay-at-home mom. This gave me lots of free time. The first year I learned French and attended lots of coffee mornings with other foreign moms, but by the second year my fingers were itching and I knew it was time to plunge back into designing or I'd go nuts. So, I went to a nearby craft store and bought some delicate wires and modeling clay, although I didn't have a clue what I wanted to do with them. The clay eventually went to amuse the kids, but the wire intrigued me. I'm not a big crocheter; all I know are the basics my grandma taught me when I was little, but somehow this felt like the right thing to do with the wires, so I crocheted a thin ring that I still have today.

I had no idea where to go from there, so I decided to find a more structured education about jewelry making. After a search, I found a small jewelry-making studio in Montreux not too far from our house, that offered a large variety of short courses. I immediately signed up for two classes, one for basic metalsmithing and the other all about wires and beading.

By the time the first day ended I knew I was home, I was so excited, like I hadn't been in years. It felt like falling in love, I was swamped with endorphins!

Out of everything I learned there, I was most intrigued by one particular stitch—and it changed my life—it was done with just a crochet hook and thin wires. We spent almost an hour in making what I now call a base (see page 24) to work from, and the next hour or so learning the stitch, and that was it.

I rushed home and couldn't stop making tube necklaces using the method. I raided all the craft stores in the area to source wires, but found a very limited selection—mostly only Christmas colors: silver, gold, red, and green, and if I was really lucky, blue. However, I worked with what I had, and made endless tube necklaces, giving them to all the moms I had coffee with—basically anyone showing the slightest interest was immediately gifted a necklace.

Then, as Christmas neared, those ladies and a few others wanted to order Christmas gifts to send home, I was amazed that people were ready to pay good money for what I was doing for fun. As a professional industrial designer, I was used to working for companies, never individuals.

On returning home to Israel, I went back to industrial design, but I wasn't using my hands and they were left itching to create actual pieces, not merely computer-generated designs. Luckily, I still had a large box filled with tube necklaces and other bits and pieces that I had no use for. Around this time my sister told me about Etsy and suggested I list them there and just see what happened. It was 2008 and Etsy was still relatively unknown among the non-arts community, also at that point I didn't know much about selling online.

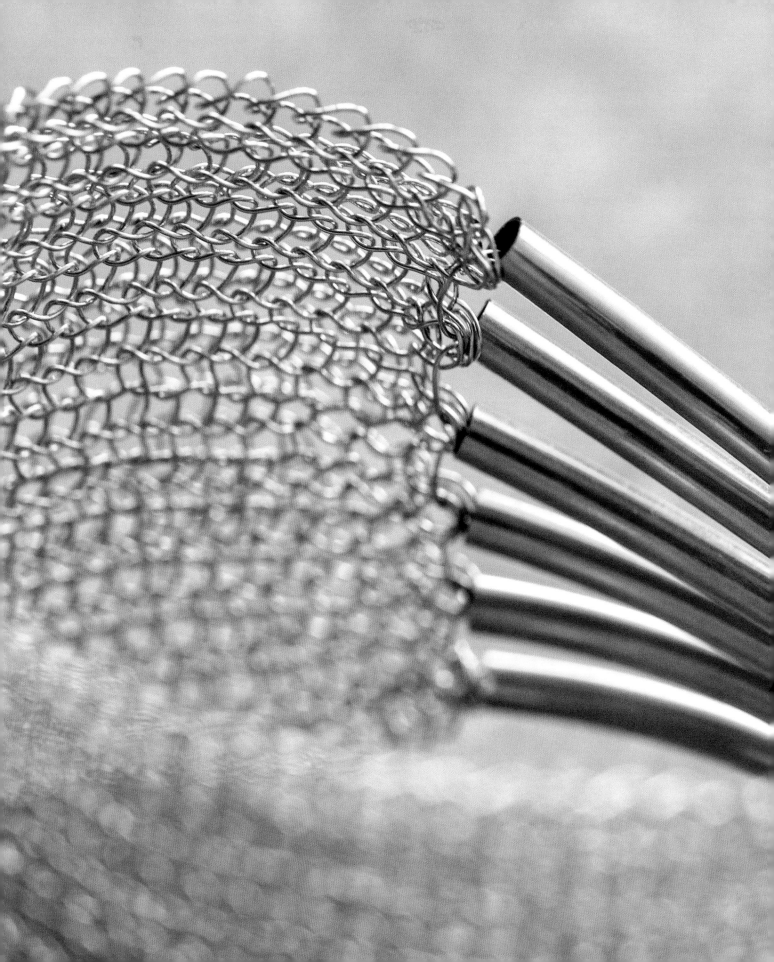

I received a warm welcome, the community loved my designs, but they were most interested in learning how I was making them (at that time Etsy was mostly a makers' collective). This is when I decided to write instructions about how I do what I do and offer them for sale along with my finished designs.

Quite a few eyebrows were raised hearing what I was planning to do; "Why would you sell your secrets, anyone could copy you?" This is all true—was, and still is—but the part that intrigues me most is the discovery stage. I'm an inventor. I like creating things. I'm less happy when I have to make more of the same; endlessly repeating the same designs bores me. I like to try something different, explore variations, and get carried away. I get a lot of satisfaction seeing my designs recreated in far-away lands, with different cultures, languages, and weather.

I love hearing how much satisfaction people get from following my techniques. For some people it helps them keep their hands busy, for others it's a true tool for pulling out of depression, and sometimes it has become a viable source of income.

My subconscious holds the keys to my inspiration. I never know when and where it will come from, I keep my channels open and welcome whatever passes through. It can be a movie, a book, a trip to an exotic place, or just life in general. Teaching, both online and in person, is also a great source of inspiration. The thought that someone is waiting there for you, to see what improvements or new designs you have come up with, is a great energy source that pulls the best out of me.

And I discovered that I really love teaching!

My design process is very intuitive and mostly achieved by experimenting. The physical requirements are minimal—just crochet hooks and wires—and the world is at my feet, anything can happen. One design leads to another, until I see the one to keep. This is why I have boxes full of samples, waiting for further development (one day) into a finished item, or just to stay as an inspiration for future designs and teaching aids.

My designs are very versatile style-wise. I have a romantic line of jewelry for brides and bridesmaids, where I combine wire crochet with Swarovski crystals or freshwater pearls. For ladies who are enchanted about the airiness of wires and want to feel unique in a minimalist way, I design clean geometric pieces, small or big, for sophisticated evening and day wear. You'll find all of these and more in the pages of this book. Enjoy!

EQUIPMENT

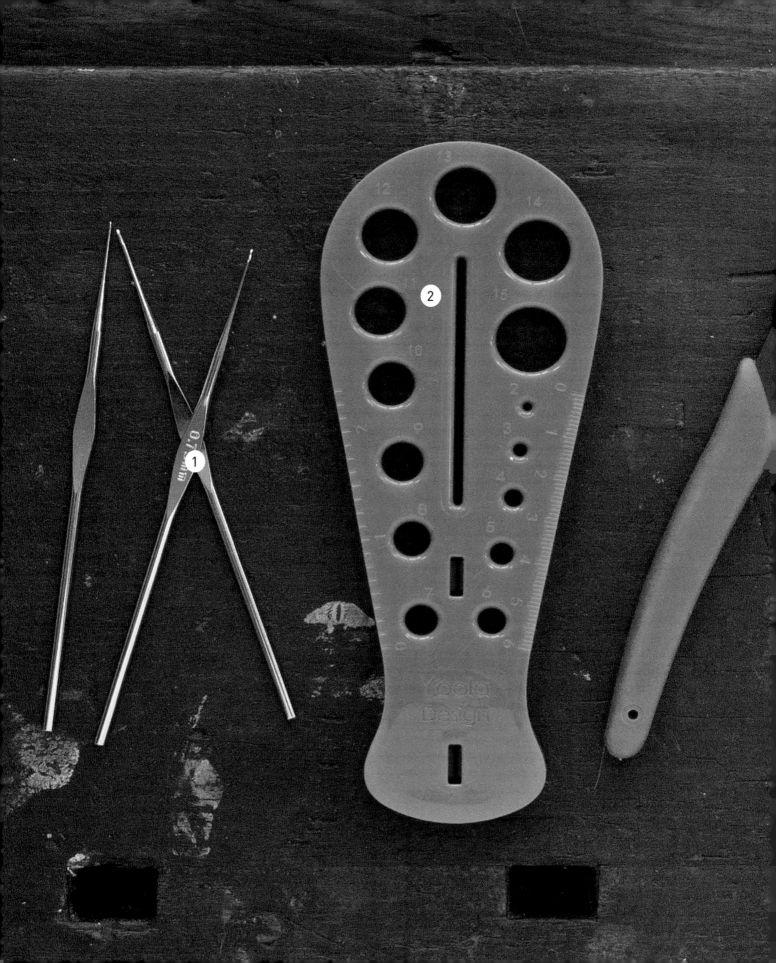

Tools

Crochet Hooks

I use the smallest size available, so usually 14 (0.9mm). Just as useful are 12 (1mm) or 10 (1.15mm). It is very important that the hooks are good quality stainless steel ones. By good quality, I mean that the hook has a smooth finish with no peeling or scratches, otherwise it will get worn out very quickly, the wire may leave marks, and the hook will not be as smooth as it was originally. It's really not enjoyable to work with a hook with flaws, it squeaks and gets stuck, the whole thing becomes a struggle instead of calm, flowing work.

Personally I started with a tiny 14 hook, and can still remember the horror when it fell to the floor and the tip broke. I then discovered it was hard to find a hook that small. As time went by and I taught more and more students both online and offline, I learned it is easier to begin with a 6/0 hook size because it is easier to pull the wire using it. But—yes, there is a but—the larger the hook, the larger its tip, which means the size of the loop needs to be large enough to pull it through. There are pros and cons here: if you use a larger hook your work can become slower because you may get stuck going in and out of the loops, but it will still look exactly the same: what determines the size of your mesh (as you will understand later on) is the diameter of the neck of the hook and not the tip. [1]

Drawplate

The drawplate is the second most important tool when wire crocheting using the ISK technique. It is a non-metallic board, with various hole sizes—knitted tubes are pulled through the holes to make them longer, smaller, softer, and denser.

My first drawplate was homemade, because I lived in Switzerland at the time and had no idea where I could source one. Jewelers' stores only have metal drawplates that will not do for this purpose. A metal drawplate is too hard for knitted wire and will more likely damage it, especially if the wires are plated. In addition we are here for fun, and its not much fun heaving around a heavy metal drawplate in your crochet bag.

So my first drawplate was a homemade one. I bought a small cutting board made of hard wood and had my husband drill holes in it. I still occasionally use this drawplate, but mainly because of the sentimental attachment. With time I learned that drawplates are also used for Viking knitting, a better-known craft then wire knitting, and other commercial suppliers already offer both wooden and plastic drawplates. These drawplates are light and relatively small and can easily fit in your crochet bag, so you always have one nearby.

As the drawplate is such a central element in the ISK tool kit, I decided to design my own. My plastic drawplate has a variety of hole sizes, plus a long slot for flat designs, measuring ruler in both inches and centimeters, and a holder for the hook. The latter otherwise tends to get lost in my crochet bag, and worse, gets stuck in textile and damages it. [2]

Wire Cutter

A wire cutter with a sharp tip is used to cut the wires and to free the work from the knitted base. Since the loops are small and delicate, it is best if the wire cutter has a sharp tip that can penetrate in between stitches and will not accidently cut your work where you don't intend it to cut. [3]

Silicon Hammer

Since we work with wires, hammering is used from time to time to harden flat pieces. The best hammer for this purpose is a silicon hammer because it will not harm the work or the color-plating of the wires. But if there isn't one to hand, you can use an ordinary hammer and protect the work with leather or a similar layer, when flattening metal. [4]

Knitting Needles

You must be wondering what knitting needles have to do with wire crocheting. Well, I use a knitting needle as a tool to stretch crocheted tubes or to form larger loops. Finally, something to do with all those lone needles ... as you don't need them in pairs. [5]

Flat-Nose Pliers

These are primarily used to assemble findings (metal jewelry pieces) and for a few other special tasks like wire wrapping, wire forming, and so on. It's important that your pliers are smooth-faced and flat-ended, so they don't have a texture that will ruin your work. Pliers come in many sizes to fit different hand sizes, but above all it's important they are comfortable. [6]

ISK Looms

A loom is not essential for ISK, but it does make things rather easier. There are many plastic looms available commercially, ranging from the smallest size with four gates for all those four-loop base projects, up to around 120 gates for really giant projects. The advantage of a loom is that it has a definite number of loops that will determine the diameter of your work, plus it is easier to hold while you work on the project. [7]

Metal Bench Block

A metal bench hammering block or small anvil is used as a base on which to hammer metal. [8]

Molds

Meshes by their nature are flexible and can usually be molded or shaped into various forms. You can use cups, vases, or bottles, and drape the mesh over open forms so you can shape them from the inner surface. Alternatively, you can also shape meshes from the outside. For example, bubbled chains are formed from the outside of a closed tube form and then forced into shape as if wearing a corset. [9]

Materials

Wires

It is crucial to use really soft wire. Wires that are not naturally soft must be treated to become soft, otherwise it is really hard to manipulate them and they might break.

Copper is a naturally soft wire and is perfect for ISK, but in its original finish it will tarnish in no time and change color from a lively orange into a dull brown. So I recommend non-tarnish wire that has been treated to keep its shade, alternatively choose a color-coated copper.

You should know that not all colored wires are copper based, some have brass hiding below the color, which results in stiffer wire that might not create the consistent result you are looking for.

Coating is also a topic to be carefully examined before investing time and effort. Quality coating will not peel while working nor afterwards. Some coated wires have a silver coat below the color. This is done in order to achieve certain shades—a nice gold shade, for example, has three layers: copper, silver, and gold.

Gold—when working with real gold, it's important to remember it needs to be soft, this is why it's not really recommended to work with 14K which is too hard. (K = karat, and indicates the quality of gold. Pure gold is 24K.) Instead, choose the softer 18K or 22K wire.

Gold-Filled—a good choice for working with a golden finish without bearing the heavy costs of working with real gold. These are gold-filled wires that have a nice golden look and are not likely to change color even with time. Gold-filled wire comes in various qualities and color finishes, the commonest being the yellow gold-filled; slightly less easy to source is the rose gold-filled. Gold-filled is available in 14/20 or 12/20 which defines what type the gold layer is made of, 12K or 14K.

Niobium—another interesting option. It is more expensive than coated copper wires and more durable, but is available in a smaller spectrum of colors. The most interesting thing about niobium is that it can come in a multicolor roll.

Silver Wire—this is a wonderful material to work with. There are two types that are best. The first is fine silver—999—very soft and delicate. The other is dead soft sterling silver—925. I emphasize the words "dead soft." If

it's not dead soft, it will not work. If you are wondering when to choose between them, keep these two simple things in mind: the 999 is very white, but very soft. For designs that need some stiffness, sterling is a better choice, but note it is a bit grayer and will tarnish quicker.

A few general things to keep in mind when working with wires:

- *Temperature affects metal flexibility and softness, especially if the wire has been stored away. In cold weather or cold environments, let the wire warm up a bit before you start crocheting—not direct heating, just room temperature.*

- *Metal hardens when force is put on it, so it's advisable to avoid stretching it—unless of course you want to harden it.*

- *My favorite tip is that wire remembers: if you bend it or wrap it, wire will remember and will tend to get back into that form. This is one of the main reasons why ISK-created work has such a lovely harmonious look, as opposed to classic crochet with wire.*

Beads and Stones

Beads and stones provide an endless selection of color and interest to ISK jewelry projects. There are a few specific rules though: when integrating them into wire crochet, the size of the holes have to be large enough for the wires to go through once—sometimes twice—and that they are in proportion to your work, beads that are too large will pop out over dramatically and tiny ones will get lost.

THE ISK
TECHNIQUE

Introduction to ISK

Invisible Spool Knitting (ISK) is my name for this technique. Despite searching masses of books, I couldn't find anything specific enough to describe the method. However, I recently managed to get my hands on a copy of Arline Fisch's book *Textile Techniques in Metal*. There she mentions something similar called spool knitting or French knitting—this is a close definition, but still not accurate. Spool knitting is done inwards and downwards, while ISK is made completely the other way—outwards and upwards.

I once had an elderly client from northern Canada who bought one of my kits to use as a bonding hobby with her mom and daughter. She realized that her grandma had taught them something similar when she was a child—they were very poor and had nothing much more than fishing wires and hooks to play with. Her grandma called it "working with angels," because it's like magic seeing the loops building up, one on top of the other, as the tube mesh is created.

Invisible spool knitting is best made using soft 28-gauge wires and a small crochet hook. This is why, although the loops look knitted, I'm more comfortable describing it as a wire crochet technique, the character of the work is closer to crochet.

The wire loops are pulled through and on top of the previous row in the round, always going right if you are right handed or going left if you are left handed. The rows build up as you progress, one on top of the other never stopping, like a spiral. Although the work is basically done in the round, there are a lot of manipulations that let you construct complex forms, flat, or with volume.

Benefits and Advantages

- ISK is a light and compact hobby; you can carry it around in your bag for those moments when you wait in line somewhere, journey on the train, and so on. You can do it anywhere provided there is sufficient light.

- The wires are an affordable material, so it's an economic hobby that doesn't require a large investment and therefore is accessible to a lot of people.

- It is very versatile for creating different shapes. I have been doing it for years, yet there is so much more to discover. ISK can create delicate minimalist designs, boho beaded styles, and fashion forward jewelry, just as easily, all using the same technique.

- The results are so neat and clean that I occasionally get asked, "are you sure this is not machine made?" Ha ha, no… its all in the technique, is my reply!

- It also has a surprisingly meditative quality; it helps calm the nerves and, as a few of my clients report, helps fight depression.

Make a Starter Row

In order to begin any ISK project you must first make a starter row—this determines the diameter of your work. The number of stitches you will need to make varies from project to project. At the beginning of each project you are told the size (ie. number) you will require. Remember, the longer your chain, the larger the diameter of your work.

The starter row can be created by crocheting a slip stitch chain or by using the ISK looms introduced in the Tools section (*see pages* 12–15).

When making the slip stitch chain I like to use U.S. size 6 (1.5mm) hook. Alternatively, use either sizes 14 or 12 (0.60mm or 0.75mm) hooks. Though, it will be slightly more difficult, but certainly possible.

Remember, the number of stitches determines the diameter of the work.

To make the slip stitch chain, use simple crochet stitches and colored copper wire. These stitches will be cut away from the jewelry when the piece is ready. For this reason, use a contrast color for this first row. For example, if your piece is in gold, choose a red or green wire.

Chain a Starter Row
Begin by making a circle with the wire and pulling a loop of wire through the circle. This is your first base loop.

Pull gently on the wire so the circle is snug at the base of the loop. This is your first stitch. (1)

Insert the crochet hook into the loop right up to the neck of the hook, then gently tighten it so that the loop size matches the hook size and the hook can pass through. [2] Bring the wire behind the loop and over the hook and pull it through the loop to make your second stitch. [3] Again, adjust the loop to match the neck of the hook. [4]

Try to keep your stitches a consistent size, not too big and not too small, ideally around ¹/₁₀" (2.54mm). If the stitches are too large, your following row of ISK stitches will fall through. If the stitches are too small, you will find it hard, if not impossible, to pull the stitches through at all.

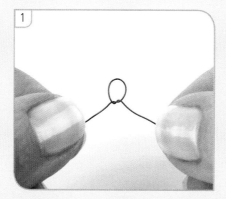

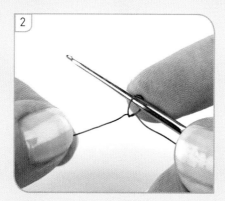

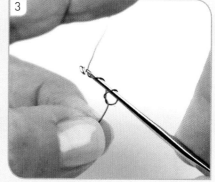

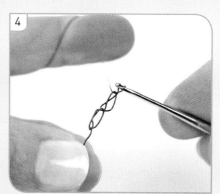

Once you have the number of stitches you need, [5] close the chain into a ring by keeping the hook in the last loop formed and sliding it into the first loop. [6]

Bring the wire over the hook and pull it through the loop, creating another loop. [7]

Cut the wire, leaving a 2½" (6.35cm) tail, and pull that through the last loop. [8]

Gently tighten it and you have a closed ring of stitches. [9] Form the ring shape with your fingers adjusting the wires so that they are all vertical. [10]

This is your completed starter row.

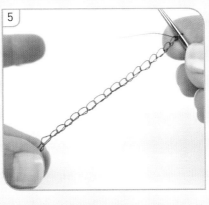

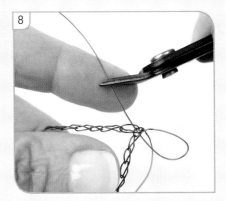

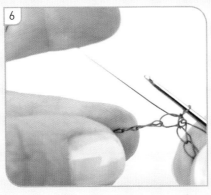

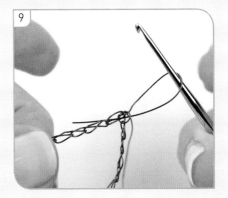

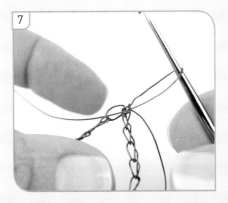

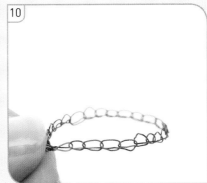

Basic ISK Stitch and Base

At the heart of each project in this book is Basic ISK Stitch. Working off the starter row, spiraling rows of ISK stitches stack to become a tube of wire that can be manipulated into a variety of shapes and patterns. The result is similar in appearance to wire Viking knit, but many find this technique to be easier and faster to work.

Essentially, ISK uses a crochet hook to pull the working wire through the stitch of the previous row. The hook itself not only leads the wire where it needs to go, but it also helps to shape each loop.

Practicing often to achieve consistently sized loops and tension will lead to beautiful, professional-quality finished designs. I also recommend creating your first ten rows of ISK in a contrasting wire and using it as a base that can later be removed and reused.

Working ISK Stitch

Insert the working wire into one of the stitches, or place it outside the ring leaving a short tail. [1]

Hold the hook facing up, insert it into a stitch in the starter row and pull the wire through from the center outwards. [2-3]

Push the hook over the starter through the newly made stitch in order to form its shape and size, push it up to the "neck" of the hook. [4]

Take out the hook and slightly bend the new stitch inwards so that it stays vertically positioned. [5]

Move on to the loop to the right (left hander's you go left,) and repeat the same action. Insert the hook, pull the wire, and push it up to the neck. [6]

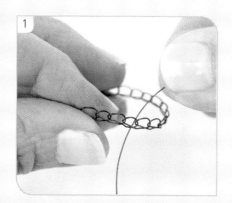

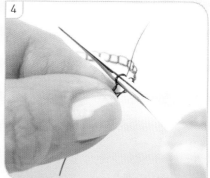

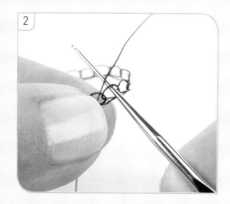

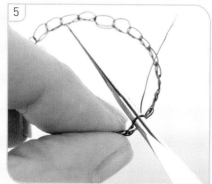

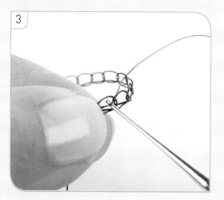

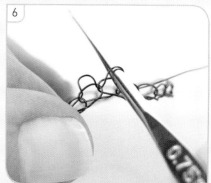

While making each new stitch hold the previous loop between your fingers so it doesn't slip open while creating the next stitch.

Continue creating loops through the original holes in your starter until you have gone around the circle approximately ten times. [7–12]

Cut the wire. These ten rows act as a base for your project. These photos show a base of twenty-four stitches, but you can make it in any number you want, but keep in mind that if you want to flatten it, there should be an even number of stitches as opposed to odd. [13]

Making A Permanent Base
If you make yourself a permanent base you can make future projects right away without having to make the chain stitch starter row. Over the years I have learned that such a base is a useful shortcut to have, and it will last for ages. If you turn the starter into a base, you will never again have to make a starter from scratch for this specific size of work. All you have to do is add a few rows to the base from time to time using leftover wire, because you snip away the top row each time you "release" a project.

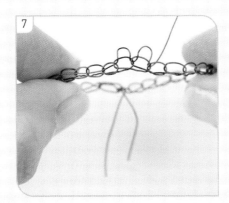

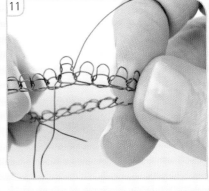

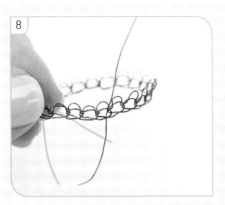

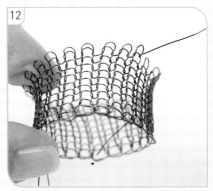

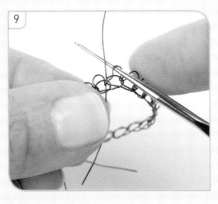

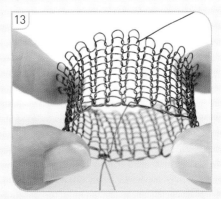

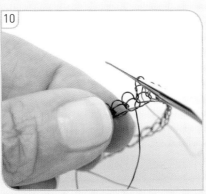

Important Pointers

The following dos and don'ts will help you achieve a beautiful, more consistent results.

Do make sure your hook is facing up, rotated only slightly to the side. [1]

Always pull the stitch straight and never rotate the crochet as you normally do with classic crochet stitches. Imagine that this is simply a hook that you are grabbing a wire with.

To successfully pull a new stitch through the loop, you need to hold the stitch of the previous row you are pulling through; otherwise it will be pulled together with your new stitch. [2]

Always push the hook right up to the neck of the new stitch, this way your work will be even, and you can work easily. [3]

Never try to catch the wire over the hook neck [4] or try and twist the hook upside down.

Push the hook up to the neck of the new stich but not over the widest part of the hook. [5]

Don't hold the wire or wrap it around your finger (as you would with yarn [6], let it feed freely into the work, no tension is required, tension will just hamper your progress. [7]

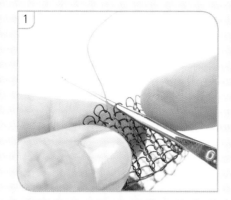

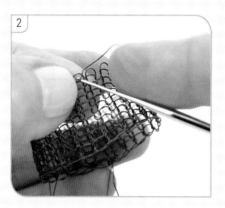

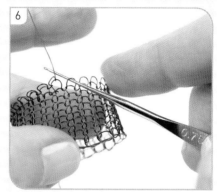

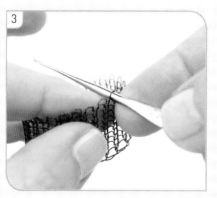

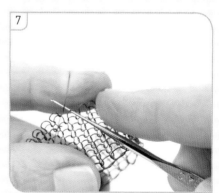

Tension

The tension of the work is determined by the spaces between the stitches, if they are very close together your work will be dense and hard, which is ideal for some designs, but a problem for others. If the spaces are too big, the work will be flimsy. The secret is to learn to control your tension and use it to the benefit of the design you are making.

An important point to note is that the tension of the work is created by where you pull the stitch from. If you pull it from close to the previous stitch [1] the result will be tight, while if you pull it from further away it will be looser. [2]

The comparison photo [3], shows two tubes crocheted with the same number of stitches by the same person. The only difference is the tension of the work. The larger tube has wide spaces between the stitches, while the narrow one has stitches very close to one another. This neatly demonstrates what a difference tension makes.

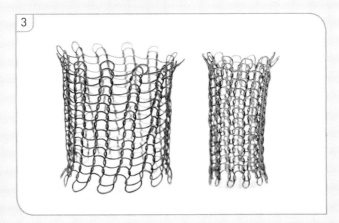

Making a Small Base

A slightly different approach is required for a base smaller than your index finger. The stitch is the same, only the way to reach it is slightly different as you can't hold the stitch between the index finger and thumb. This makes projects with smaller bases considerably trickier.

For a four-stitch base: create a starter made of four loops in exactly the same way as for the twenty-four base starter (*see pages* 22-23). [1]

Insert the hook into one of the stitches and pull a new working wire from the inside to the outside of the loop ring through the loop. Push the hook through the new stitch in order to form its shape.

Take out the hook and slightly fold the new stitch so it stays in place and doesn't split open. [2-3]

To make this easier, you can insert a knitting needle of the same gauge into the starter ring to open it up a little.

Move along to the loop to the right and repeat the same action, holding the work like a flower stem. [4]

Keep working in the same direction until you have gone around the circle about ten times. The rows will build up like a spiral. Cut the wire leaving a short tail. [5-8]

Your four-loop base is ready. [25]

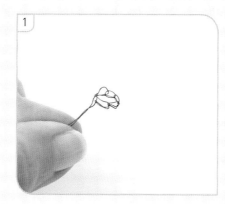

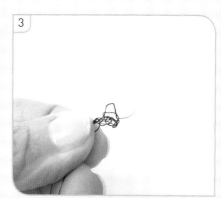

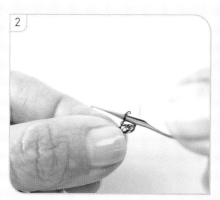

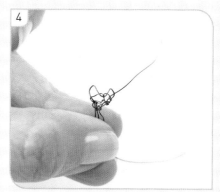

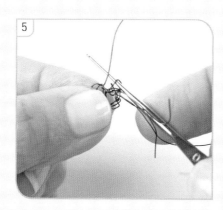

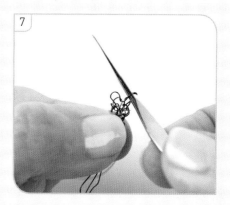

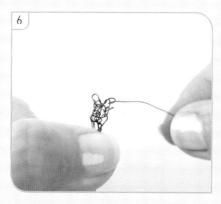

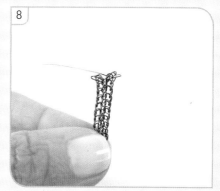

Using a Loom

When making a base with an ISK loom, the loom itself acts as your starter row. You'll use the holes in the loom, called gates, as if they were the stitches of a starter row.

With your working wire, slide the wire through a gate on the loom from the center towards the outside leaving a short tail. [1]

Insert the hook into the gate to the right [2] and pull the wire from the center to the outside through the hole, [3] the hook should be pointing up. Once gone through the hole push the hook through the new stitch on top of the ISK "top" until it goes through the widest part for the hook, this will form its size. [4–6]

Take out the hook and slightly fold the new stitch inwards so it stays vertically positioned. [7]

Move to the next gate on the right, and repeat the same action, make sure to hold the new loop with your left hand fingers while pulling the next stitch, this will ensure it doesn't slip open. [8–10]

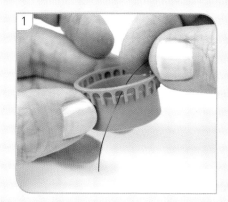
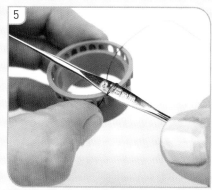
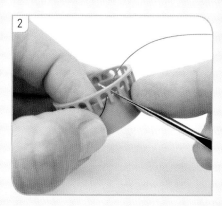
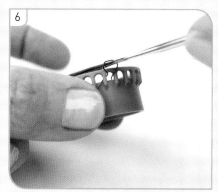
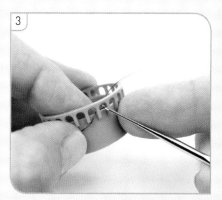
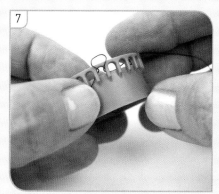
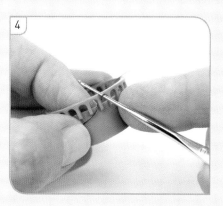
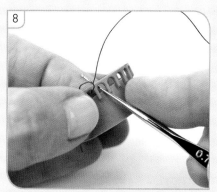

Continue in this manner until each gate has a wire stitch. [11]

For the second row and onwards, work the Basic ISK Stitch (see page 25-26). [12-18]

Whether using an ISK loom or a wire crochet ring as your starter row, the resulting ISK stitch base has the same appearance. [19]

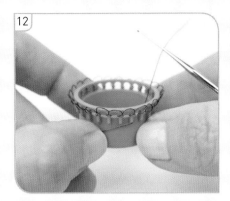

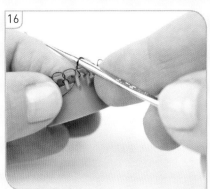

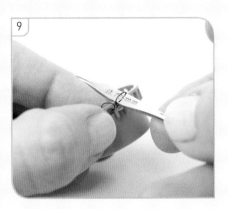

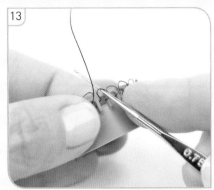

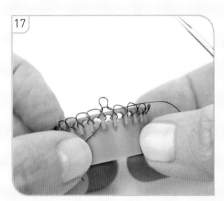

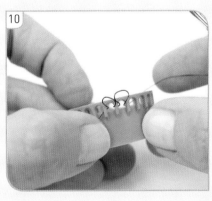

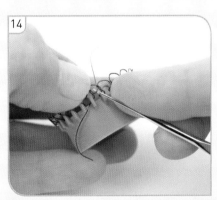

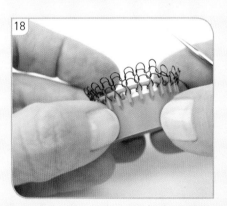

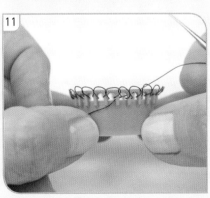

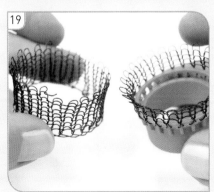

Decreasing Stitches

In the ISK method, the number of stitches in a round are decreased (or reduced) by inserting the hook into two or more adjacent stitches instead of just one, and pulling a new stitch from there.

Decreasing can be made selectively, at regular intervals, or all around a given row.

To make decreasing easier, break the process into two steps: start by bringing the two or more stitches together so their holes align. [1] Once they are in complete alignment, pull the new stitch through. [2]

Adding Stitches

I always recommend starting large and reducing, rather than adding stitches, but in some cases it is unavoidable.

When adding stitches its important to do it gradually, and not increase too many stitches into the same row unless you want a dramatic increase in size. If too many stitches are added all at once the work will become deformed and you might loose control over the shape altogether.

Stitches are added by pulling a new stitch out from between two existing stitches. [1-4] For best results, there must be sufficient space between them; they can't be too close together.

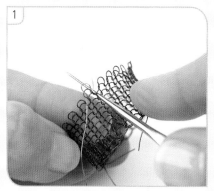

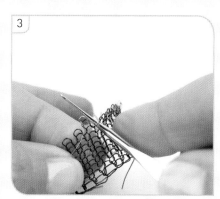

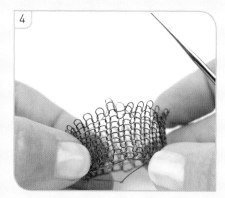

Loop Hem

To maintain the "loop look" at the end of a knitted piece with an open end, fold each loop over the matching one on the row below it. This will maintain the look of the open loops at the same time as securing the stitches so they don't ravel.

Insert the hook into a stitch loop. [1] Bend the hook towards the inside center of the piece, bending the loop with it. [2] Continue around the piece bending the other loops inward. [3] Fold the stitch inwards, securing the stitch.

Note: Do not bend the stitch loop outwards as that cause the look to slip through the loop below. [4]

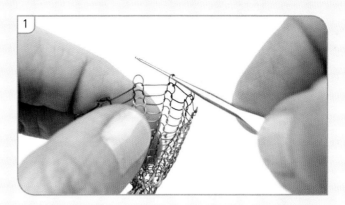

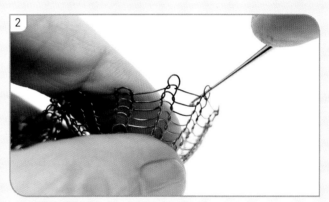

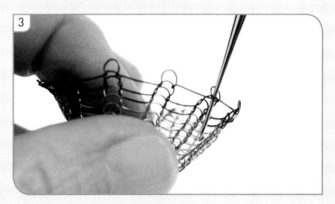

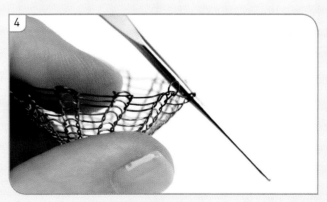

Flat Stitch

When a flat hem is wanted, we do a flat stitch. It results in a look similar to a bind off edge in knitting. This is made the same way as the Basic ISK Stitch with one major difference: you don't take the hook out of the stitch to make a new one.

Flat Stitch in the Round

To begin flat stitch, pull a loop through the next stitich. [1] Keep the hook in the stitch and drag it with the hook over to the next stitch [2], then pull the wire through both loops [3]. Do this until a full row is created [4].

Note: To prevent the stitches from becoming too dense and gathered too closely together, it's important to drag the stitch to the next one, and not just align them both together.

Flat Stitch on Flattened Tube

The flat stitch can also be made after a tube has been flattened. This is done exactly as explained above but with one difference, you grab the stitches after going through stitches from both sides of the tube and not just one side [5-8].

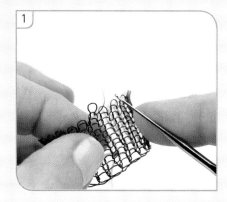

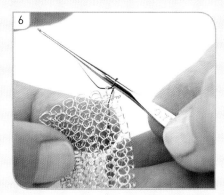

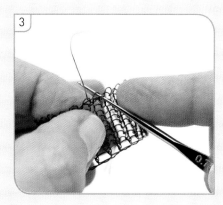

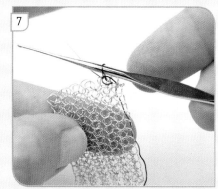

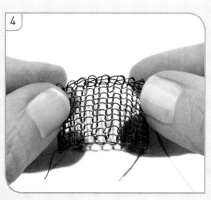

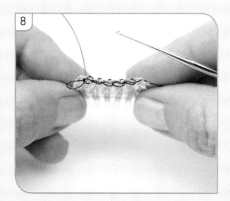

Wire Ends

When working with wires it is most important to avoid sharp ends that can be painful against the skin. It helps to hide those ends within the hollow of the work whenever possible. If working flat, those ends must be more cleverly hidden. It is best to hide the wire end between stitches where they are held under some tension, normally two wraps will do the job.

Traditionally, wire should be snipped with a sharp flush cutter and filed smooth if sharp before tucking it into the work. However, if you don't have access to tools, you can use the "pull and twist" method, in which you pull the wire close to the point you want it to break [1] and twist it round and round until it breaks. [2] The wire may still be sharp. You can use a basic emory board nail file to remove any sharp points.

Changing Wires

Wires occasionally need to be changed, either because the wire has run out in the middle of the work, the wire broke—yes this can happen, not very often but it does—or the wire color needs changing.

Once you get the idea you'll realize it's not that complicated and new wires can blend quite nicely into the work. To elegantly hide the wire change, ISK works with the advantages of wire.

I often get asked in disbelief, "This is it? Won't it split open? I don't need to tie a knot or anything?" The answer is simple: "No." The wire is locked in place and, if cut as explained below, will be unfelt and unnoticed.

To change wires, crochet two stitches (only two!) with the old and new wire together, as if they were one [1–4], then continue working the round with just the new wire [5].

After another row or two, cut the tails short from inside the work. [6] Continue working in the round with the new wire. [7-8]

Note: Its important to cut the tails as short as you can with the wire cutter. The direction is important, as well. By directing it inwards the ends are unlikely to stick out or catch on the outer surface.

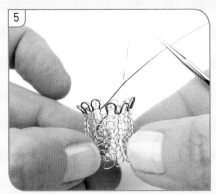

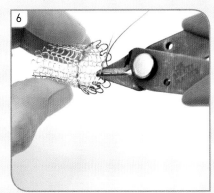

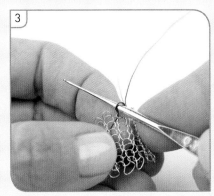

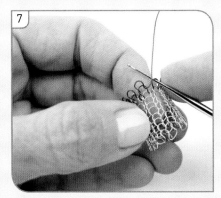

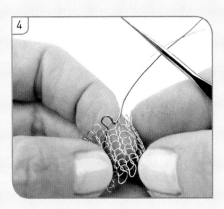

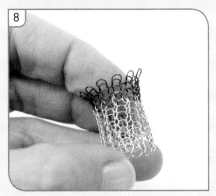

Pulling Back Work

Sometimes you need to undo a few rows. In that case simply pull them carefully inwards to the center of the knitted tube and they will split open. Don't pull them one by one outwards, this will put the wire under too much stress and might cause it to break.

Releasing from the Base

To release the work from the base, cut off the last stitch of the base—this should be in a contrast color and therefore easy to identify. Go into each stitch making extra sure you cut only that stitch and not a piece of your work. To help avoid mistakes, I recommend you count the stitches, this way you know you went into each and everyone of them.

Use flush cutters and cut each horizontal line of wire between each stitch around the tube. This is clearly seen when using contrasting color for the base as shown. [1–3]

Once you have cut all the stitches, gently pull the components apart and they will split away from one another. [4–6]

Remove any remaining small pieces of wire and the base is ready for a future project.

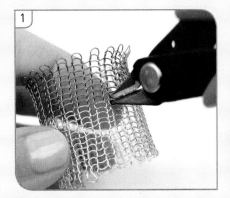

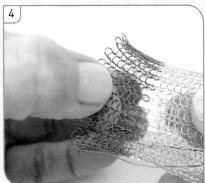

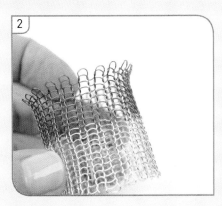

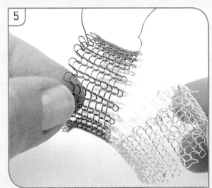

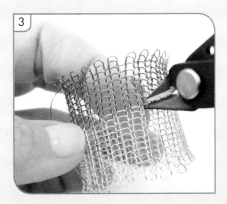

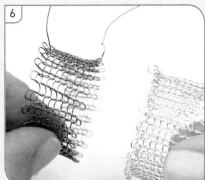

Adding Stiffness

Occasionally the work can become too flimsy and floppy, which can be a problem for some projects. There are remedies. Flat flowers can be work-hardened by hammering them with a plastic hammer against a metal block, [1] but make sure to protect them with a piece of leather first. Also, overenthusiastic hammering can damage soft wire and cause them to cut into one another.

Tubes can be hardened by pulling them through a drawplate. (See photos on the facing page.) At first they will become flexible, which shouldn't be confused with softness, but as you work it through decreasingly smaller holes, the work becomes denser, harder, and less crushable.

Another method of hardening ISK tubes is to insert a knitting needle down the throat of the crocheted tube. The needle has to be larger than the tube. This will make the tube less flexible. [2]

To harden dimensional designs that aren't tubes or surfaces, use a mold. [3–4] Drape the work over a suitable mold to enlarge it, gently stretch it, and make it stiffer in the process. I used this method when I make pendant light shades—not just to make them stiffer, but also to make sure they are all the same size.

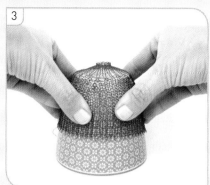

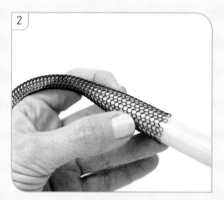

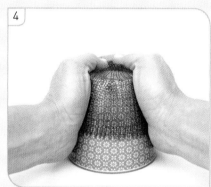

Using a Drawplate

ISK tubes can and should be drawn through a drawplate to create an even and a smooth-looking tube.

Begin by drawing the tube through a hole relatively near the same diameter as the tube you've made. [1–2]

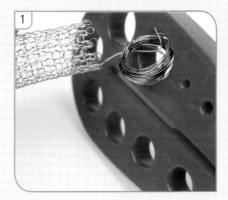

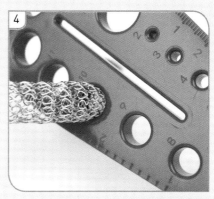

Continue pulling the tube through ever decreasing size holes until you reach the desired diameter of tube. [3–6]

Note: At some point the tube will become so dense that it can no longer pass through the holes, but you should stop the process well before you get there: if the tube is too hard it will lose its flexibility and will no longer drape nicely.

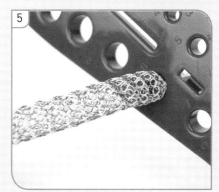

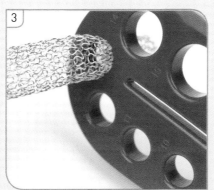

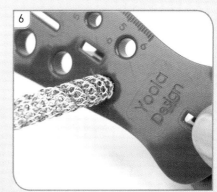

Flattening Designs

As you probably realize by now, my whole world of ISK is created in the round, even the flat looking designs such as rings, necklaces, and bracelets. Crocheting them in the round gives them a dense looking texture when flattened in the finishing process. This flattening is a delicate, calculated manipulation—absolutely don't confuse it with crushing!

So that your flattening looks consistent and elegant, the tube needs to go through some preparations. Obviously the more even your stitches and spaces are, the easier it will be to flatten your tube.

Don't pull the knitted tube through a drawplate before flattening. Depending on the effect you want, insert a knitting needle of a slightly smaller or slightly larger size than your tube. If the tube is too large for the needle you could use several needles together. Stretching the tube like this will give you a clear view of the stitches and will enable help you flatten the tube evenly.

The thing that gives the flattening tube its most significant feature are its edges/rims, so it's important that a consecutive row of neat stitches is picked to function as the rim.

Step 1

Begin flattening from the side of the crocheting where you stopped, not from where you began. Carefully arrange the loops from both sides in pairs. [1–2] Start by creating a rim on one side of your tube, and then move over to the other side. [3–5]

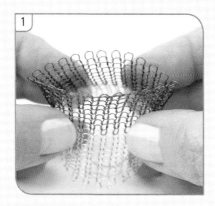

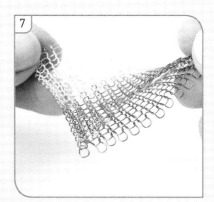

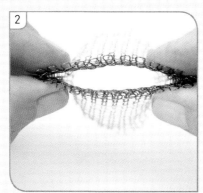

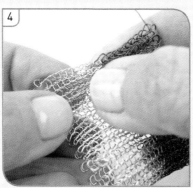

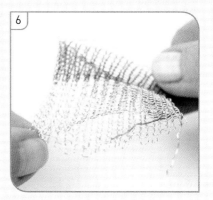

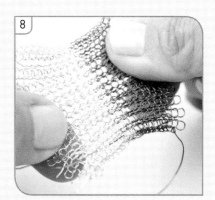

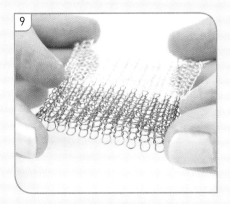
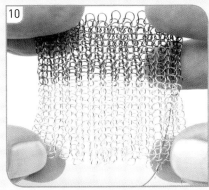

Step 2

Once the two rims are visible the strap can be stretched to give the flat designs a nice textile-like and even look. [6–10]

You can also use a slot to flatten the tube evenly.

Sculptural Objects

It shouldn't come as a surprise that non-tubular elements are also made in the round. This just requires some imagination during the crocheting process.

Step 1

Several tubes can be merged together, [1–4] or branches can be crocheted out from the side of a tube [5] and so on.

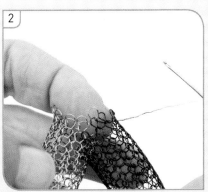
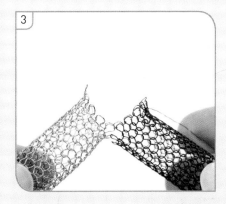

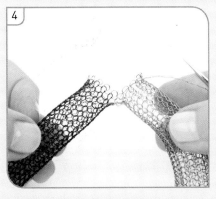

Interweaving Beads and Stones

Wires occasionally need to be embellished to add color or detail. For this beads and small pretty stones can be used to great effect, although personally I like to keep them to a minimum. I prefer the bare look of the construction of the wires. However, in the right color, shape, and size they can work magic.

A huge variety of beads—glass, stone, metal, crystal— can be incorporated and woven into ISK wire crochet work in a number of different ways. The only requirement is that they have a hole big enough to freely accommodate the 28-gauge wire we use, or in some cases two wires.

One of my favorite methods starts with stringing all the required beads for the project onto the wire prior to starting the work, and then caging them in between stitches as the work progresses. [1–7] This method ensures a fine clean finish, but requires pre-planning. If the beads are smaller than the loops, they can be threaded inside the loop itself and not necessarily pre-threaded.

Beads can also be stitched to the work at a later stage by weaving them into the project. Just think of your crocheted mesh as a canvas and use a wire in the same color you crocheted with.

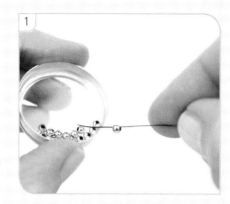

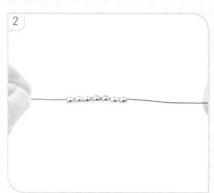

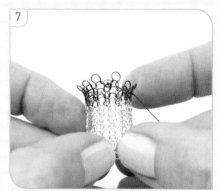

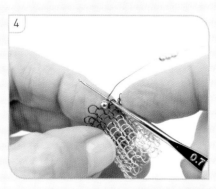

Stitch Size

Stitch size is an important topic with ISK wirework. Changing the size of your stitch can increase or decrease the size of your work without adding or removing stitches. The easiest way to handle this is to use the size of the crochet hook neck/handle. To achieve consistent stitches, always insert the hook up to a specific point. I don't recommend swapping your crochet hook for a different size.

Insert the crochet hook into a stitch to pull a new one. {1}

Only push the tip of the crochet hook into the stitch do not push up to the neck as you would in a regular size ISK stitch {2-3}

Note: *This takes practice to master.*

Larger stitches are another option, but are only recommended for advanced users, as the stitches slip out of larger stitches very easily. For this to work you need good control of the tension of the whole project.

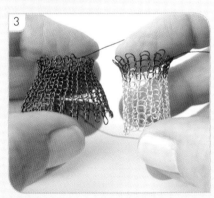

Insert the crochet hook into a stitch to pull a new one creating a large loop. [4]

Using a knitting needle with a larger diameter than the crochet hook, insert into each new stitch immediately after it has been created. This will ensure your stitches are the same size. This can only be done as you progress. [5-7]

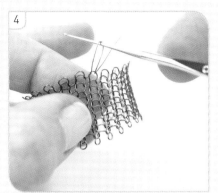

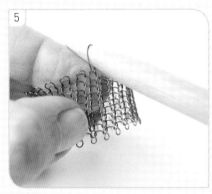

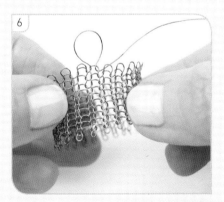

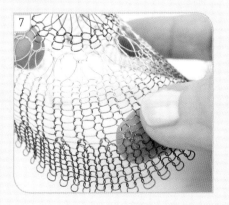

One-Layer Mesh

ISK is traditionally worked in the round. However, there are times when you may want to work flat to create a single layer of ISK mesh.

There are two methods to working one-layer mesh. The first creates texture in keeping with stockinette stitch in knitting, the second produces something similar to garter stitch with slightly raised ridges.

Method 1 - Stockinette Stitch

Row 1: Work the set number of stitches from left to right across the work. When you reach the desired point, stop and wrap the working wire along the right edge of the last stitch made.

Row 2: Draw a new stitch through the last stitch of the previous row and work across the designated number of stitches from right to left.

Continue repeating rows 1 and 2 until the mesh is the desired length.

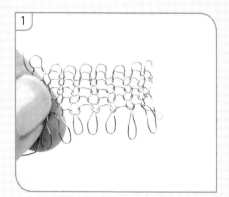

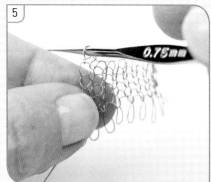

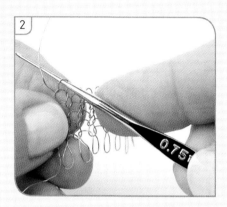

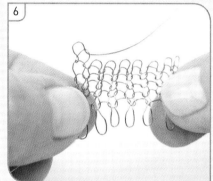

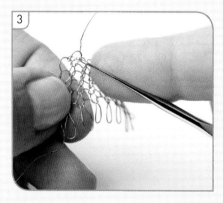

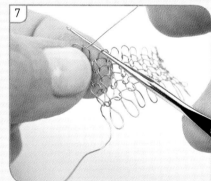

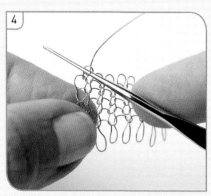

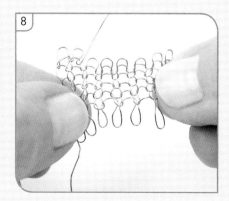

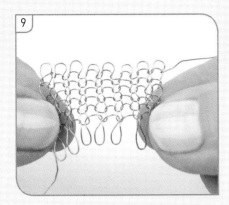

Method 2 - Garter Stitch

Row 1: Work the set number of stitches from left to right across the work. When you reach the desired point, turn the work so you're looking at the back of the mesh. Wrap the working wire around the piece so it is in position to work the next stitch.

Row 2: Work in Basic ISK Stitch from left to right across the row. When you reach the end of the row, turn the work to the front, wrap the wire so it's in position to work the next stitch of the next row.

Repeat rows 1 and 2 until the mesh is the desired length. [1-12]

Note: These two options will have slightly different results. Stockinette stitch gives a more uniform mesh, but with some distortion to the edges. Garter stitch creates subtle ridges on each side of the work with a much cleaner outside edge. [13-14]

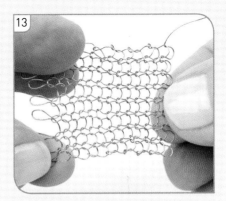

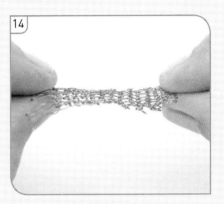

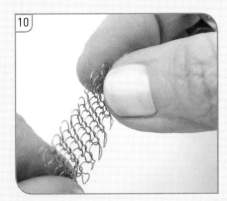

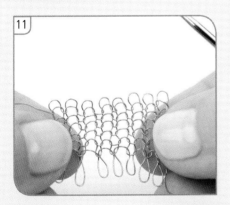

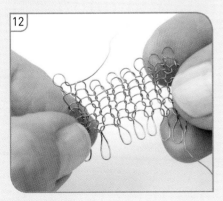

TIPS AND TROUBLESHOOTING

Tips

The following are a variety of tips and information I have picked up over the years.

Wire spool location

Where you put the spools you are working with matters: if you are right-handed place the spool slightly to the right and never to the left. This enables the smooth and continuous feed of wire onto your hook. If you have your spool on the left you will feel a slight resistance in the wire as it gets hooked, and even small nicks.

Left-handed people should do the opposite and keep their spool slightly to the left, as this smoothly feeds the wire in the direction of the work.

Left-handers

In almost every group I teach there is at least one left-handed person. One interesting thing I often hear from left-handed class participants is the comment, "I'm left-handed but I can also work with my right hand, I prefer to first try working like everybody else." However, almost always after a few attempts, they switch to working with their left as the leading hand.

Left-handers should work exactly the opposite way to how I explain the work (to right-handers), meaning the hook should be held with the left hand, the work with the right hand and most crucially, they should work to the left, in a clockwise direction, and not counterclockwise like right-handers.

Most left-handers manage to teach themselves to craft by translating the right-handed instructions (I expect they are used to it). However, I managed to teach myself to demonstrate with my left hand as well, and believe me this is not obvious at all, but it's a great lesson for two reasons. Firstly, you actually feel your brain burst into flames sending your hands instructions, and secondly, it reminds me of the difficulties all beginners feel in making their hands do what their mind tells them to do.

Spool in a zipper bag

When working with more than one spool of wire, or if your wire is "jumpy," it's useful to place the wire in a plastic zipper bag or container of some kind while working to keep the wire under control.

Lighting conditions

The wires used in this craft are fine and delicate and so is the hook, this is why really good lighting conditions are absolutely essential. The best light is natural light, but if this is not possible perhaps because you work at night or the natural light simply isn't bright enough, make sure to work in a well-lit place.

Seeing aids

Seeing what you do in wire work is even more crucial than when working with yarn or cotton. When you crochet with wire you have to see every detail. Sometimes my students realize it's time to start wearing glasses or update the strength of their existing ones. Inadequate seeing aids can lead to a frustrating experience and poor progress. I always keep glasses in a variety of strengths in the studio and I've seen the miracles it does when people are finding learning difficult. When they see what they are doing sharply, they succeed!

Additional seeing aids such as a magnifying table light, magnifying trays, or jewelers magnifiers can also be useful.

Your hands

Your hands are just as important as your eyes, so don't get over excited and stress them, they might react poorly. The ISK, as opposed to classic wire crochet, does not need the wire to be under any tension, so the work should not hurt your hands or stress them.

Nevertheless, let your hands rest from time to time. Stretch out your fingers and wriggle them and remember to give your hands a break every so often. Hands are not little machines, they are your hands, they are important!

Neck and shoulders

It's very personal but what isn't … as when crocheting your head is bent downwards, you should remember to move your neck and shoulders occasionally or you will end up with a stiff neck and aching shoulders. Take a break and walk around a bit every so often and move them both.

Troubleshooting

Over the years, and with the many students I have had, I think I have seen everything that can go wrong when learning ISK. Here are some of the most common problems.

"My tube becomes conical"

This is something I see quite often. There are two causes: firstly, some people naturally tend to pull the already knitted loops outwards, and this pulling grows and gets worse as the work progresses. The second cause are large spaces between the loops, or what I call problems with the tension of the work. The spaces in between stitches are as important as the stitches themselves, yes, the stitches need to be round and uniform, but if the spaces between them are not even, the work will not have a uniform look, and the tube will be deformed.

The remedy is to avoid pulling the stitches against the direction of the work. Also, be careful to keep the spaces even between your stitches to make sure everything is uniform. If you notice a change in the tube, adjust it by gently pulling and pushing: do this every couple of rows until you are happy with the results.

"My loops slip open"

This mostly happens because the loops are too large, so the stitches easily slide out. Remedy this by pushing the wire right up to the neck of the crochet hook. If you want to make larger loops, it is possible, but this requires a higher level of control over your work. One way to bypass this situation is to give the stitches a slight inward fold with every stitch as you work.

"My loops look like narrow slits, rather than round like yours"

Slit-like loops are the consequence of the hook crushing the row beneath the one you work on. When a new stitch is made you should be hovering over the row beneath, rather then leaning on the previous row. Once you avoid this habit, your loops will start looking round and pretty, I've seen this correction work numerous times..

"My tube became hard and it doesn't stretch when I flatten it"

Hard tubes can still develop even if you work with the correct wire gauge and softness. It is the consequence of loops being too tightly squeezed together without space between the loops. The work becomes dense and looses its flexibility—this being said, some designs benefit from the effect, while others suffer—the key thing is to understand why it happens, and learn to control it. Enlarge the space between the stitches by pulling the wire further away from the previous loop.

"My loops are not even"

Uneven loops are the commonest concern for beginners. The ultimate trick to making even loops is to always push the crochet hook right up to its neck in the wire loop. Also, be consistent with the angle you push the hook through and pull the loops.

However, remember that some inconsistencies will disappear once you have stretched or pulled the crochet through the drawplate. Depending on the design you are making, this happens because there are no knots along the work, the loops are all open and connected to one another, so some wire will seem as if it has moved from one stitch to the next. This is adjusted back in the stretching.

"My work tends to spiral"

Mine too … this happens as a consequence of the angle you pull your stitches. If the angle points towards the center of the work, the stitches will be straight, but if your stitches point to the right, your work will swirl.

But this can be an advantage, thanks to this fact I came up with the infinity necklace design. Because my stitches had this spiral about them I decided to take it to the extreme instead of fighting it, and came up with a design that enhances it!

When making lattice designs the twisting will disappear when you strengthen and stretch the design. In general it tends to be more visible in smaller designs than large ones, where you have more control over the angle at which you pull the stitch.

But if you want to either tame it or enhance it, at least now you know how.

STEP-BY-STEP
PROJECTS

Asymmetric Elegant Bracelet

The Asymmetric Bracelet is an elegant accessory with a luxurious look that resembles an evening dress with one bare shoulder.

Finished Size
Width: approx. 1.5" (4cm)
Circumference: adjustable.

Difficulty Level
Beginner

Techniques Used
Basic ISK Stitch and Base Tension
Releasing from the Base
Flattening Designs
Flat Stitch

Tools
U.S. size 12, 14, or 10 (0.75, 0.6, or 1mm) crochet hook
Base of 24 stitches
Plastic spacer slightly larger then the length of tube beads
Wire cutter

Materials
60' (18.2m) 28-gauge dead soft wire

Findings
Six curved metal tubes 2.5 x 30mm

Step 1

Leaving a tail of 8" (20cm) and working on a base of 24 stitches, ISK stitch approximately eight rows. [1]

Step 2

Release the crocheted tube from the base. [2]

Step 3

Continue wire-crocheting simple ISK stitches until you have reached around 65 rows. With average working tension this should be a cuff size of 7" (18cm). [3]

Step 4

Flatten the tube, and make sure to fold the edges neatly. [4]Step 5 Holding both ends, stretch the strap. This makes it smooth and even, if you have a drawplate with a slot, use it to pull the tube through. [5]

Measure the strap; it should be 6 ¾" (17cm) for cuff size 7. If it's too long, open up and remove a few rows from the bottom side (the side released from the starter). If it's too short, open up the top end, shape it back into a tube form and crochet a few more rows. Repeat Steps 4 and 5 until it is the desired length.

Step 6

Insert the hook into two stitches from both sides of the folded strap; you should have a total of four stitches on the hook. Wrap the wire around your finger and pull a stitch through the four loops. Pull the stitch to make it larger [6], then insert the spacer to set the correct size of stitch. [7]

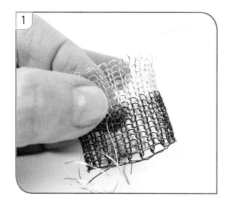

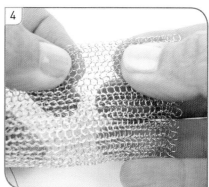

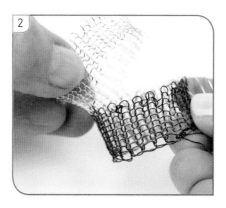

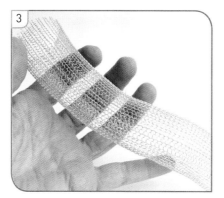

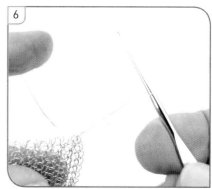

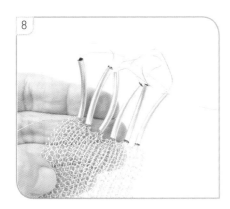

Step 7

Take out the spacer, string a tube bead onto the elongated stitch, and insert a hook or a toothpick to hold the bead in place. Do the same to the additional five tube beads — hold them all together with spare wire or a safely pin. [8]

Step 8

Time to connect both ends. Rotate the bracelet to continue working with the wire left on the side released from the starter. Insert the hook into four loops, two from each side of the strap, and the stitch popping out of the tube bead (five stitches total on the hook), and then pull a stitch. [9] Without removing the hook from the new stitch, drag it to the left picking up the next four stitches plus the stitch popping out of the next tube bead, and pull a stitch. [10] Continue in the same way until you connect all six tubes.

Step 9

Trim excess wire and tuck ends. [11]

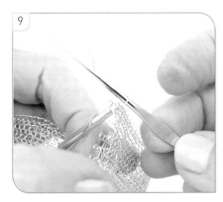

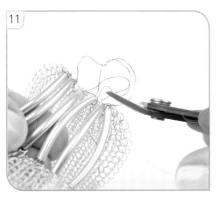

Boho Wrap Bracelet

Wrap bracelets are super easy to make and can be formed in endless color combinations. The design is simple, yet versatile, and can go all the way from boho to minimalist simply by choosing different shades.

Finished Size
Three wraps: 25½" (65cm) long
Four wraps: 35¼" (90cm) long

Difficulty Level
Beginner

Techniques Used
Basic ISK Stitch and Base
Releasing from the Base
Using a Drawplate
Changing Wires

Tools
U.S. size 12, 14, or 10 (0.75, 0.6, or 1mm) crochet hook
Base of 12 stitches
Wire cutter
Drawplate

Materials
88' (26.8m) 28-gauge dead soft wire, 3 colors; 56' (17m) main color, 14' (4.3m) each accent color
Rapid glue gel

Findings
One ¼" (7mm) magnetic tube clasp

Step 1

Leaving a tail of 4" (10cm), using ISK stitch and base of 12 stitches, wire crochet one row of regular stitches in the main color (shown here, gold). [1]

Step 2

Using color 2 (shown here, ultra white), leave the same tail of 4" (10cm) and pull a stitch, [2a] then before taking out the crochet hook, pull a second stitch on top of it using the gold wire. [2b] You have just created stacked stitches in two rows. This is the method you use for making the whole bracelet.

Step 3

Continue working as in Step 2, pulling the next stitch in color 2 and working a stitch of main color on top. [3]

Note: The unique spiral stitch of this design isn't visible until you pull it through a drawplate.

Tip: If you don't have patience and want to see that the texture is actually showing up, you can do Step 5 before completing 72 rows. The number of rows may vary according to your work tension and the size of the wrist you are making the bracelet for.

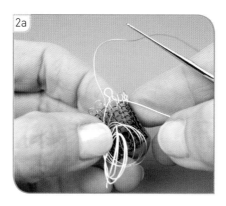

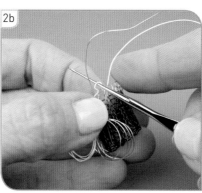

Step 4

After ten rows, release the knitting from the base, and continue wire crocheting until you have made approximately 36 rows of each color.

Step 5

Without cutting the wires, insert your crocheted tube into the drawplate: start with a hole similar to the size as your tube. Pull the tube all the way through, then insert it back into the same hole to pull it all the way back. [5]

Note: This is done because the spools are still connected to your work.

Continue drawing the tube through decreasingly smaller holes until you have gone through a hole of ¼" (7mm). Measure to see if it comfortably goes around your wrist once. If not, widen the end and crochet a few more rows: if it's too long, carefully open up a few rows and pull them back.

Step 6

Cut the wire for color 2, leaving a few inches. Join a second spool of the main color by placing the wire parallel to the tail of color 2 just cut. Make two stitches with the tail of color 2 and the new main color as if they were one, crochet a stitch on top of the stitches just worked using theoriginal main color wire. Continue working around as in Step 2. [6] After two rows, cut the tail wires from inside the tube.

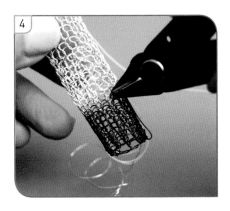

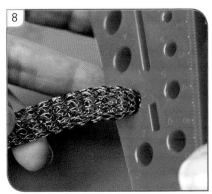

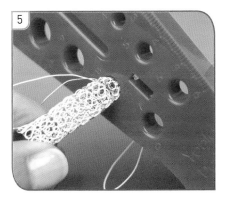

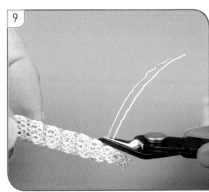

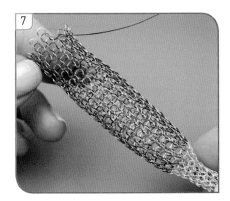

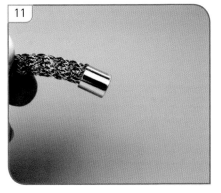

Step 7

Continue working Basic ISK Stitch until section 2 is approximately the same length as in Step 2. Repeat Step 5 drawing the tube through the drawplate. Repeat Step 6 changing wires to introduce color 3. this time into magenta. [7]

Step 8

Continue working section 3 as per the previous sections. Draw the whole chain through the drawplate. Measure to check that it wraps around your wrist three times. [8]

Step 9

Secure the end wires and cut them short. [9]

Step 10

Insert the chain ends into the tube clasp to check that it sits comfortably inside. Use rapid glue gel on the crocheted tube end and attach the clasp. [10-11] Repeat to attached the opposite end of the clasp.

Cleopatra Cuff

The Cleopatra Cuff is an impressive royal piece of jewelry. It's not difficult to make, but because of its size, it does require quite a bit of stitching. As implied by its name, the design is inspired by the Ancient Egyptian Queen Cleopatra.

Finished Size
Width 4" (10 cm) wide
Circumference adjustable

Difficulty Level
Advanced Beginner

Techniques Used
Basic ISK Stitch and Base
Releasing from the Base
Tension
Flattening Designs
Decreasing Stitches
One-layer Mesh

Tools
U.S. size 12, 14, or 10 (0.75, 0.6, or 1mm) crochet hook
Base of 48 stitches
Wire cutter

Materials
115" (35m) 28-gauge dead soft wire

Findings
One 8-row magnetic tube clasp

Step 1
Leaving a tail of 98" (250cm),using ISK stitch and base of 48 stitches, wire crochet eight rows. [1]

Step 2
Carefully release the knitting from the base. [2] Continue working Basic ISK Stitch until you have approximately 62 rows in an average tension.

Step 3
Flatten the tube and stretch it. [3]

Step 4
Working from the end of the tube with the long tail, pull up one stitch before decreasing in one-layer mesh as follows to adjust the width to the clasp. [4]

1st row: decrease two pairs of stitches at each end—a total of eight reductions. This leaves you with 20 stitches on each side.

2nd row: decrease another two pairs of stitches at each end—a total of eight reductions. This leaves you with 16 stitches on each side.

3rd row: decrease two pairs of stitches at each end—a total of eight reductions. This leaves you with 12 stitches on each side.

4th row: decrease only one pair of stitches at each end—a total of four reductions. This leaves you with ten stitches on each side.

5th row: decrease only one pair of stitches on each end—a total of four reductions. This leaves you with eight stitches on each side.

Step 5
Measure the cuff to see if it fits. Keep in mind that the claps will take another $1/3$" in (1cm) or so. If it's too short, keep on crocheting

for another few rows at each end. If it's too large, release a few rows evenly from each end.

Step 6
Repeat Step 4 at the other end of the cuff to mirror the first end.

Step 7
Leave a tail of 6 $1/3$" (16cm) and cut the wire.

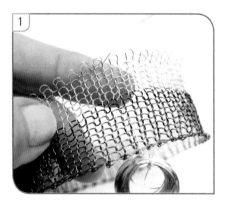

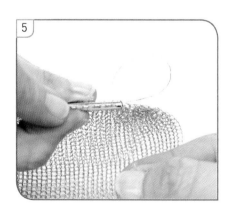

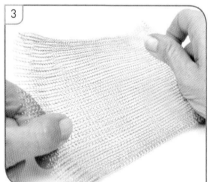

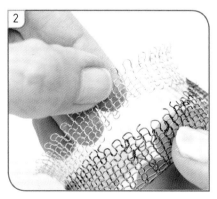

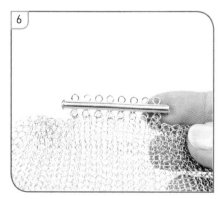

Step 8

Assemble the clasp as follows:

- Insert the clasp like a sandwich in between the two sides of one of the cuff's ends.
- Using the wire, connect the two sides and the clasp together. Thread the wire in and out of all eight loops in one direction and then all the way back. [5-6]
- Wrap the wire twice in a dense spot and cut it short.

Step 9

Repeat Step 8 at the other end of the cuff being careful to assemble the other half of the clasp in the right direction. [7]

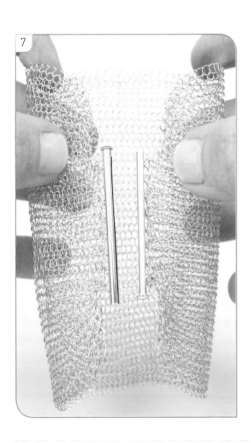

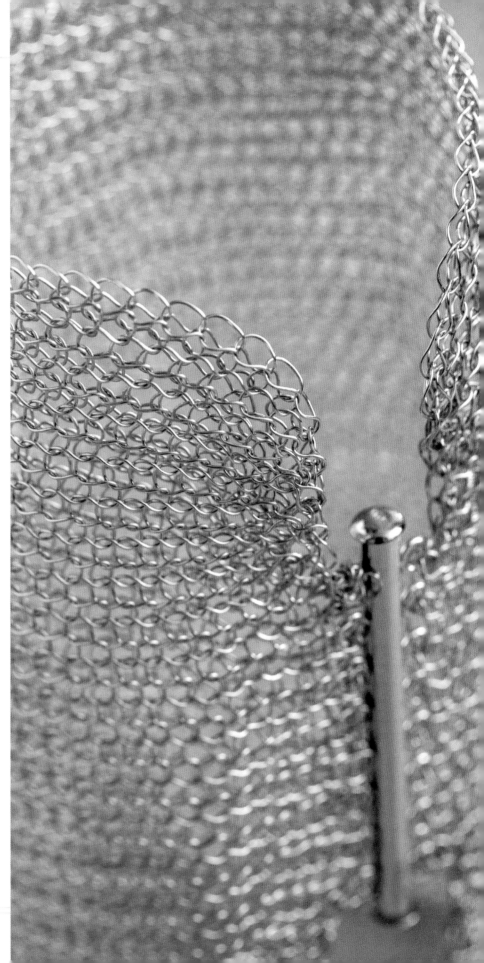

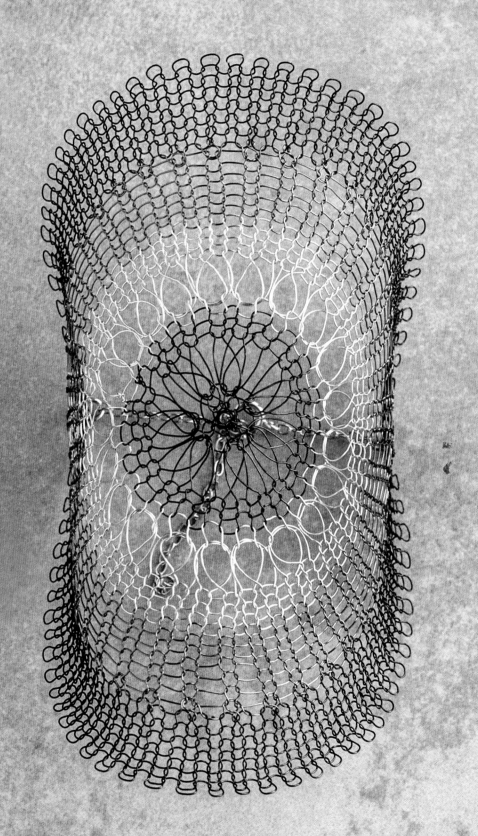

Tattoo Statement Bracelet

This large yet delicate design makes a bold statement with subtle, beautiful texture.

Finished Size
Center piece: 6" (15cm) diameter
Circumference: adjustable

Difficulty Level
Intermediate

Techniques Used
Basic ISK Stitch and Base
Releasing from the Base
Changing Wires
Decreasing Stitches
Stitch Size

Tools
U.S. size 12, 14, or 10 (0.75, 0.6, or 1mm)
crochet hook
Base of 84 stitches
Wire cutter
Flat-nose pliers
U.S. size 11 (8mm) knitting needle

Materials
46" (14m) 28-gauge dead soft wire, 3 colors.

Findings
One spring ring clasp
4¼" (10.5cm) chain, divided into 2 lengths,
1" (2.5cm) and 3¼" (3cm)
Two jump rings

Step 1
Leaving a tail of 2" (5cm), use Basic ISK Stitch and a base of 84 stitches, crochet seven rows with color 1. [1]

Step 2
Change wires to color 2 and crochet one row of ISK stitch. [2]

Step 3
Work one row of decrease stitches around the row; when finished, 42 stitches remain. [3]

Note: Start holding the work from the bottom to allow the work to shrink toward becoming a dome.

Step 4
Crochet another regular ISK stitches row.

Step 5
Release the knitting from the base and flatten it. [4]

Step 6
Crochet another four rows of regular ISK stitches. [5]

Step 7
Change wires to color 3 and crochet three rows. [6] If the work deforms, hammer it on both sides with a silicon hammer.

Step 8
Crochet one row of large stitches using a U.S. size 11 knitting needle. [7-8]

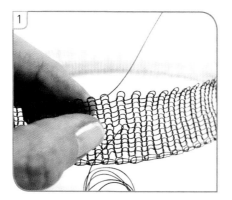

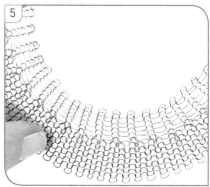

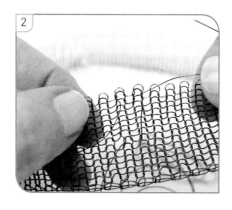

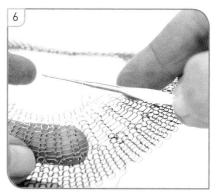

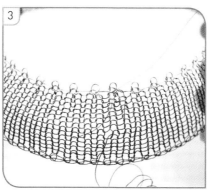

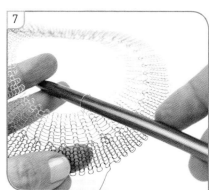

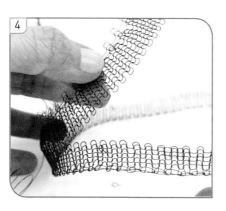

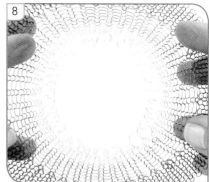

Step 9

Work a round of decrease stitches decreasing every two large stitches into one. Before working each subsequent decrease, crochet a second stitch in color 1 on top of stitch just worked. [9-10] At the end of the round 21 stitches remain.

Note: This technique makes it easier to crochet on top of the large stitches. If this is not done, the stitches tend to fall through and open up.

Step 10

Crochet one round of Basic ISK Stitch with color 1. Trim color 3 and tuck the tail into the work. [11]

Step 11

Crochet a row of large stitches as in Step 7 with color 1. Then pull each stitch tip towards the center using a crochet hook—this will give them a pointy look. This can be done after the creation of each loop, or when you finish going around making all the large loops of this row. [12]

Step 12

Decrease every 3 large stitches into 1 using the same method as in Step 9; 7 stitches remain. [13-14]

Step 13

Decrease every 2 stitches until 4 stitches remain.

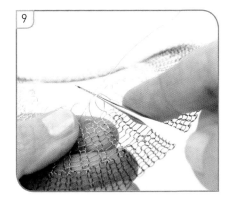

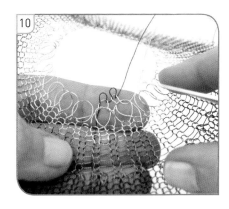
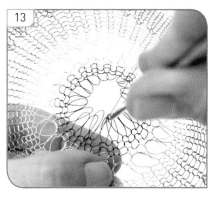
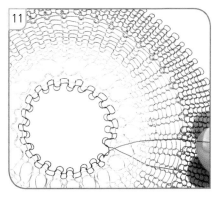
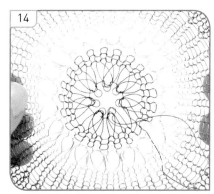

Step 14

Using the hook, place the 4 stitches one on top of the other to create a center. Trim the working wire 2" (5cm). Thread the wire tail through the center of the overlapped stitches and wrap the stitches to hold them together. Cut excess wire and tuck in the end. [15-17]

Step 15

Examine the entire component for ends where colors were changed. Be sure to trim all ends flush and tuck into the work. Leave the starting tail of wire as is.

Step 16

Place the first and second stitches on the outer skirt of the work one on top of the other. Using the tail available, wrap the stitches together with the wire. This is where you will connect the clasp or chain.

Step 17

Create similar merged stitches on the opposite side of the work using a short scrap of color 1.

Step 18

Attach the 1" (2.5cm) chain with a spring ring clasp at one end to one of the merged stitches formed in Steps 16 and 17. Attached a 3" (8cm) chain on the opposite merged stitch. [18-19]

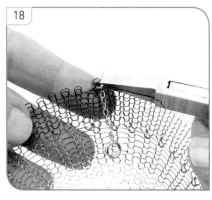

Friendship Love Bracelet

This bracelet is a delicate and romantic piece of jewelry, particularly appealing to young people. It looks great in one color and even better in two. It's a one-size pattern, with the size adjusted using the clasp.

Finished Size
Length: 8" (20cm)

Difficulty Level
Advanced

Techniques Used
Basic ISK Stitch
Making a Small Base
Releasing from the Base
Using a Drawplate
Decreasing Stitches

Tools
U.S. size 12, 14, or 10 (0.75, 0.6, or 1mm) crochet hook
Base of 4 stitches
Wire cutter
Flat-nose pliers
U.S. size 1 (2.5mm) knitting needle
Drawplate

Materials:
9¼' (2.8m) 28-gauge dead soft wire, each of 2 colors

Findings
One spring ring clasp
Extension chain
Two jump rings

Step 1
Leaving a tail of 3" (8cm), wire crochet approximately 60 rows of ISK stitches with color 1 on the four stitch base. [1]

Step 2
Release the work from the base. [2]

Step 3
Use a U.S. size 1 (2.5mm) knitting needle to even out the work. [3]

Step 4
Pull the tube through a drawplate starting with a 5mm hole size. [4] Gradually draw through smaller holes until you reach the desired diameter. You should end up with a tube of about 7" (18cm) long.

Step 5
Decrease the stitches at each end into one stitch. Then cut the wire leaving a tail of 2¾" (7cm).

Step 6
Hold the two end loops together and wrap the wire around them both to make a hanger loop. [5] Cut the wire short. Wrap the other short tail twice and cut it short.

Step 7
Repeat Steps 1-6 to create a second piece in color 2. [6]

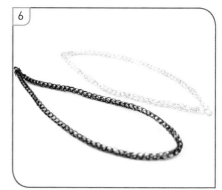

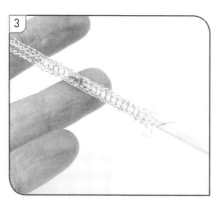

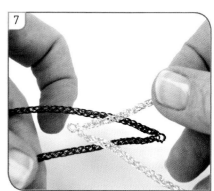

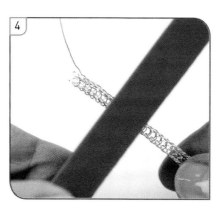

Step 8

Place the two pieces on top of each other with the tips pointing towards one another. Pull the ends through the loops of the opposite piece until they are locked together in a tight knot. [7-9]

Step 9

Attach the clasp on one end and the extension chain on the other using jump rings.

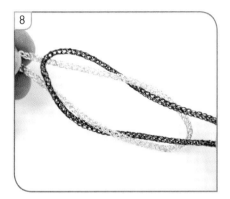

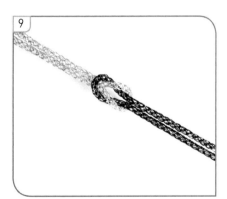

Long Tube Pearl Necklace

Sometimes the most basic design is the most elegant of them all—a simple long tube necklace with pearls freely swinging through it.

Finished Size
Length: 30" (75cm)

Difficulty Level
Beginners

Techniques Used
Basic ISK Stitch and Base
Releasing from the Base
Using a Drawplate
Decreasing Stitches

Tools
U.S. size 12, 14, or 10 (0.75, 0.6, or 1mm)
crochet hook
Base of 12 stitches
Wire cutter
Flat-nose pliers
Drawplate

Materials
120' (36.5m) 28-gauge dead soft wire
Fifty five 8.5mm pearls

Findings
One spring ring clasp
Extension chain
Twp jump rings

Step 1

Leaving a tail of 8" (20cm), use Basic ISK Stitch and a base of 12 stitches, crochet eight rows. [1]

Step 2

Release the knitting from the base. [2]

Step 3

Continue wire crocheting until you have 8" (20cm) of wire remaining. [3]

Step 4

Pull the crocheted tube through the drawplate, starting with a hole similar in width as the tube. [4] Continue passing the tube through decreasingly narrower holes until the piece passes though a $^3/_8$" (10mm) hole.

Measure the tube to check it has the overall length is 30" (75cm). If it's too short, open up the end and crochet additional rows; if it's too long, carefully open up a few rows.

Step 5

String the pearls on a wire. [5]

Step 6

Push the pearl chain into the crocheted tube until it reaches the other end, you can use the crochet hook to tease it forward if it needs assistance. [6-7]

Step 7

Decrease one end of the chain until 2 stitches remain. Wrap the wire neatly over both stitches to create a loop for the jump ring, make sure the wire supporting the pearls still pops out. [8]

Step 8

Repeat Step 7 at the other end.

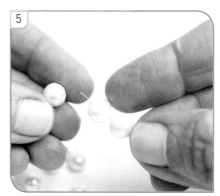

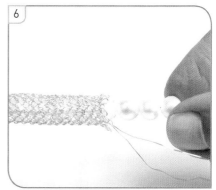

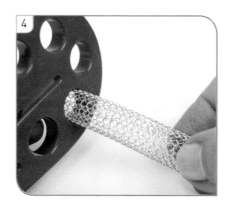

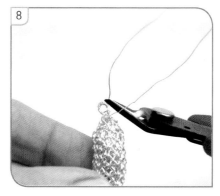

Step 9

Adjust the pearl wire to make sure the pearls lie where you want them in the chain. Secure both ends to the end loops you created in Steps 7 and 8. [9]

Step 10

Attach the spring ring clasp and the extension chain to either end of the necklace with jump rings. [10]

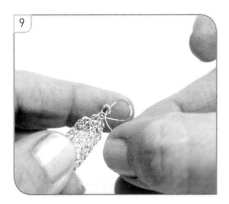

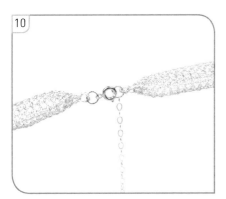

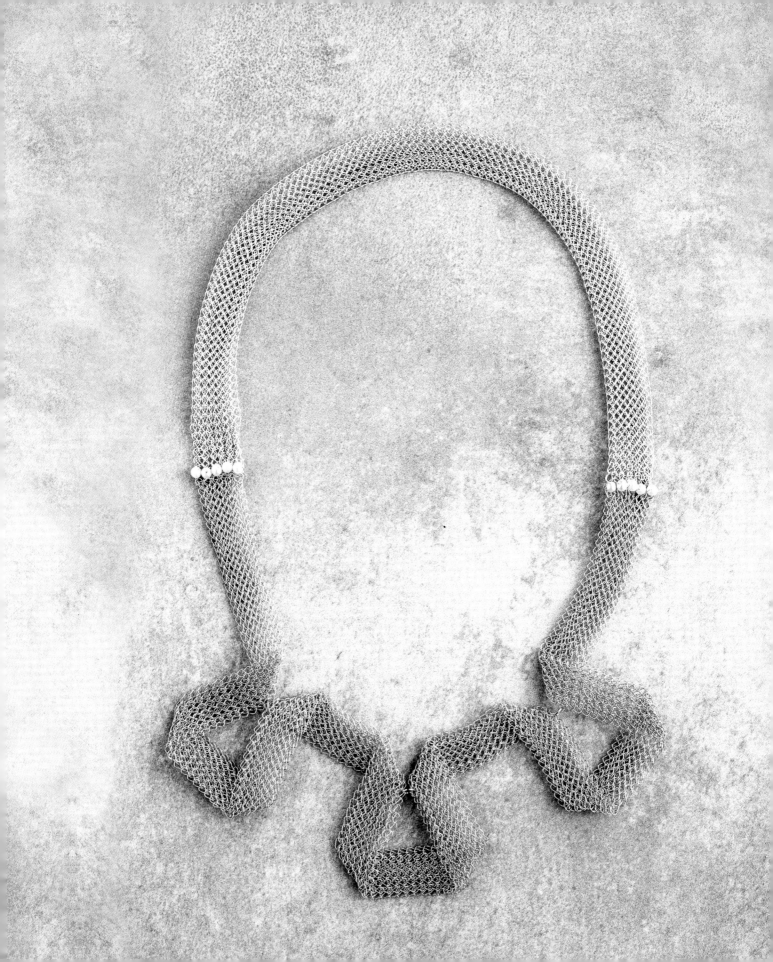

Origami Necklace

The Origami Necklace, as its name implies, incorporates similar folding techniques as used in paper origami.

Finished Size
Length when folded: 23½" (60cm) long

Difficulty Level
Beginners

Techniques Used
Basic ISK Stitch and Base
Releasing from the Base
Flattening Designs
Flat Stitch
Interweaving Beads and Stones

Tools
U.S. size 12, 14, or 10 (0.75, 0.6, or 1mm)
crochet hook
Base of 12 stitches
Wire cutter
Flat-nose pliers
Plastic card 1"x 1¾" (2.5 x 4.5cm)

Materials
120' (36.5m) 28-gauge dead soft wire, each
of two colors
Ten 3mm pearls

Findings
Four jump rings

Step 1

Leaving a tail of 8" (20cm), use Basic ISK Stitch and a base of 12 stitches, crochet ten rows with color 1 (gold). [1]

Step 2

Release the knitting from the base and continue wire crocheting until you have about 21 $^2/_3$" (55cm). [2]

Step 3

Following Steps 1 and 2, prepare a second tube with color 2 (silver) color. Make it approximately 13" (33cm) long.

Step 4

Flatten the ISK tubes, stretch them to make them flexible and about $^2/_3$" (1.5cm) wide. [3]

Step 5

Measure the straps. After stretching, color 1 (gold) should be 23 $^2/_3$" (60cm) and color 2 (silver) should be 14" (36cm) long.

Step 6

Mark the center of the gold strap with contrasting thread. [4] Place the center of plastic card on top of the gold strap aligned to the mark. Fold the strap to create a 90-degree angle on either side of the card. [5]

Step 7

Turn the folded strap over, and using the full width of the card, make a third fold and its mirror fold. [6-9]

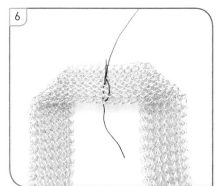

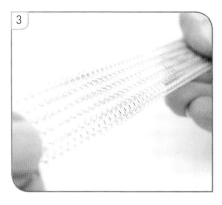

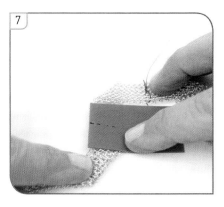

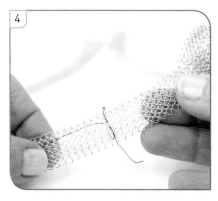

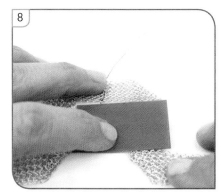

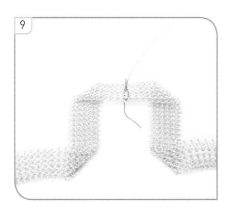

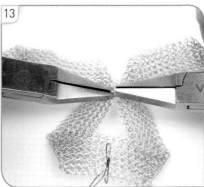

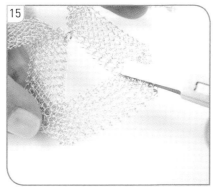

Step 8

Turn the strap over again and using the card to ensure that your pattern is even and aesthetic, create an additional two folds. [10-12]

Step 9

After a total of 12 folds, there should be three distinct U shapes in the strap. Using flat-nose pliers and jump rings, pull the corners of each U together. [13-14]

Step 10

Using the flat-nose pliers, press each section to harden the folds. [15]

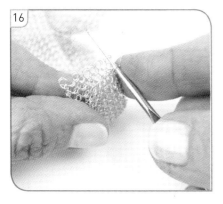

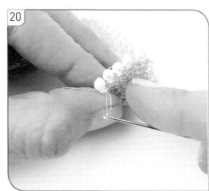

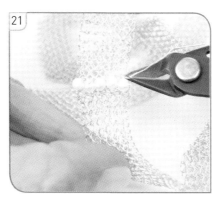

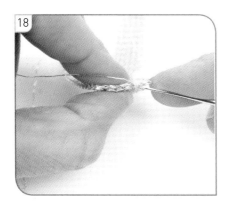

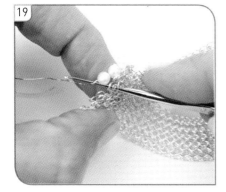

Step 11

Join color 1 and color 2 straps together with beaded wire as follows. Hold both strap ends parallel to one another with the tail you intend to crochet with to the far right. String five pearls on the wire tail. Insert the hook into four loops and pull a stitch, [16] leave the hook in the stitch andpush a pearl up to the stitch just worked. [17] Work the next pair of stitches together. [18] Continue until you have connected all 6 pairs of stitches with five pearls locked in place. [19-20]

Step 12

When you reach the end, secure the wire through the last loop. Wrap the wire twice around the work and trim short. [21]

Step 13

Repeat Steps 11 and 12 to connect the other end in the same way, but make certain that you are connecting it in the same direction so that the pearls show on the same side.

Modern Cloud Bib Necklace

A Modern Cloud Bib Necklace in two colors is a bold piece for stylish ladies looking to make a statement with their appearance.

Finished Size
27½" (70cm) long

Difficulty Level
Beginner

Techniques Used
Basic ISK Stitch and Base
Releasing from the Base
Changing Wires
Flattening Designs
Flat Stitch

Tools
U.S. size 12, 14, or 10 (0.75, 0.6, or 1mm)
crochet hook
Base of 12 stitches
Wire cutter
Flat-nose pliers

Materials
120' (36.5m) 28-gauge dead soft wire, each
of two colors

Step 1

Leaving a tail of 8" (20cm), use Basic ISK Stitch and a base of 12 stitches, crochet ten rows with color 1 (purple). [1]

Step 2

Release the knitting from the base and continue wire crocheting until 4" (10cm) of wire remains.

Step 3

Change wire to color 2 (silver). [2] Continue working until approximately 14½" (37cm) of the color 2 remains. Cut the wire leaving an 8i" (20cm) tail.

Step 4

Flatten the crocheted tube. If needed, stretch it very lightly. This design iis most successful if the work isn't too flimsy and has some hardness. [3-4]

Step 5

Using the length of color 1, form three gentle overhand knots with the strap. Be careful not to kink the strap as you work. The strap should flow smoothing through the knotting. When you reach the end of the shade, pull the remaining strap through the last loop. [5-7]

Step 6

Lay the necklace on a flat surface. Hold both strap ends parallel to one another and align. [8]

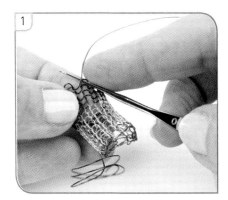

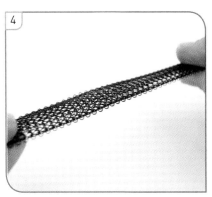

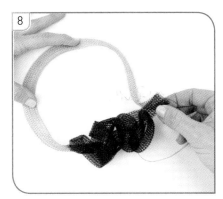

Step 7

Using flat stitch, connect the two strap ends. [9]

Step 8

Press the joined ends using flat-nose pliers. [10]

Step 9

Wrap both wire tails twice and cut them short. [11]

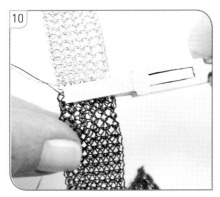

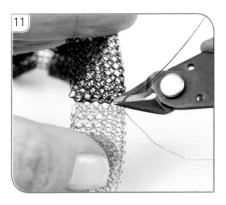

Stone Charm Pendant

Stone pendants, with all the unique energies they bring to their wearer, are a winning piece of jewelry, easily adjusted to any stone's shape or size.

Finished Size:
Length: 1¾" (4.5cm)
Width: 1" (2.5cm)

Difficulty Level
Beginner

Techniques Used
Basic ISK Stitch
Making a Small Base
Tension
Releasing from the Base
Using a Drawplate
Decreasing Stitches
Stitch Size

Tools:
U.S. size 12, 14, or 10 (0.75, 0.6, or 1mm) crochet hook
Base of 8 stitches
Wire cutter
U.S. size 8 (5mm) knitting needle

Materials
2 ⅓' (70cm) 28-gauge dead soft wire
One 25-35mm round cabachon

Findings
Necklace chain, desired length

Step 1

Leaving an 8" (20cm) tail, work Basic ISK Stitch around a small eight stitch base for 36 rows using average tension. [1]

Step 2

Release the crocheted tube from the base.

Step 3

Flatten the tube and stretch it. If available, pull through a slotted drawplate. [2-3]

Step 4

Place the crochet mesh around the stone, then shape it with your fingers to follow the stone's profile. [4]

Step 5

Remove the stone from the mesh. Decrease the stitches at both ends of the strap until you have 2 loops on both ends: a total of 4 loops. Enlarge the loops using a knitting needle. [5-6]

Step 6

Cut the wire that is still connected to the spool leaving a tail of 8" (20cm). Return the cabachon to the crocheted frame. Thread the tail wire through either side of the strap starting next to the four loops moving forward towards the stone until it holds it very firmly in place. [7-8] Wrap the wire twice and cut it short.

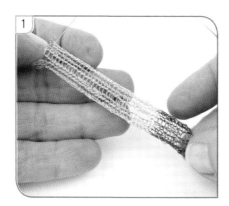

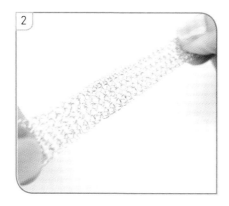

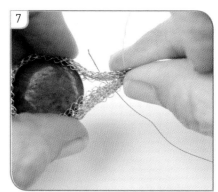

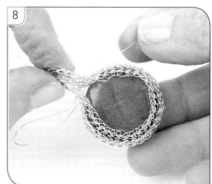

Step 7
Use the remaining wire to wrap the four large loops together to create a bail for the pendant. [9]

Step 8
Thread a length of chain through the bail. [10]

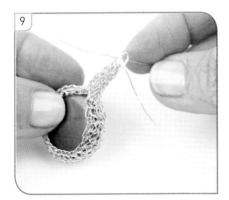

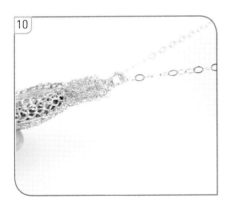

Floral Statement Necklace

A fun, eye-catching colorful floral necklace, worn over the head.

Finished Size
Length: 33" (85cm)

Difficulty Level
Intermediate

Techniques Used
Basic ISK Stitch and Base
Releasing from the Base
Changing Wires
Using a drawplate
Loop Hem

Tools
U.S. size 12, 14, or 10 (0.75, 0.6, or 1mm)
crochet hook
Base of 12 stitches
Wire cutter
Drawplate

Materials
90' (27.4m) 28-gauge dead soft wire, each of
two colors
4 $\frac{2}{3}$' (1.4m) 28-gauge dead soft wire,
contrasting color

Step 1

Leaving a 60" (150cm) tail of color 1 (gold), make one stitch. Without taking the hook out, work another stitch with color 2 (white) leaving a short 2" (5cm) tail. Continue working in this way, making two rows simultaneously with two colors unitl ten rows are worked. [1–2]

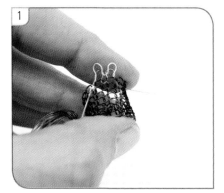

Step 2

Release the knitting from the base, and continue wire crocheting until you have made about 130 rows of each color. [3]

Note: The number of rows may vary according to your crochet tension.

Step 3

Insert your crocheted tube into the drawplate, starting with a hole of a similar width as the tube. Draw the tube all the way through. Continue pulling it through decreasingly narrower holes until pulled through a hole of ¼" (7mm). [4]

Note: Check to make certain that the chain can go over your head because there is no clasp in this design. If it's too short, open up the end and crochet as many more rows as you need. If the necklace is too long, carefully open up a few rows to shorten its length.

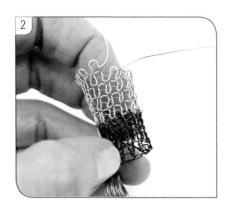

Step 4

Secure the wire end of color 2, and cut it short from the inside of the tube. Stretch the end of the tube outward to create a cone shape. Then continue working with color 1 work eight rows. [5–7]

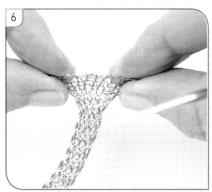

Step 5

Change wires into the contrast color and work three rows while continuing to work out in a funnel shape.

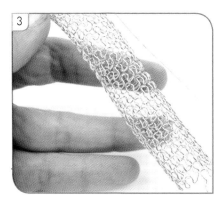

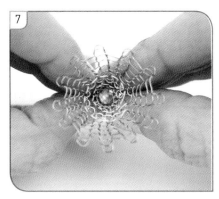

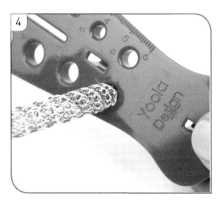

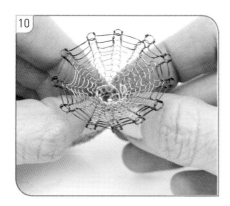

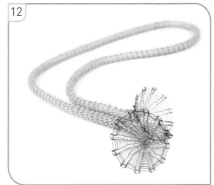

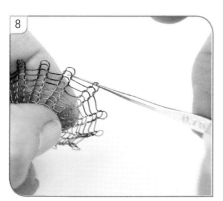

Step 6

Secure the wire and cut it short from the inside of the flower.

Step 7

Insert the hook into the top stitch and fold it inward working a looped hem. [8-9] This secures the end stitches and stops them opening up.

Step 8

Create an identical cone flower at the other end of the tube. [10]

Step 9

Secure the tubes together using a scrap length of wire. [11] Trim excess wire and hide end. Bend and shape the flowers to make them curve forwards. [12]

Bold Hoop Earrings

These Bold Hoops are a truly timeless, classic piece of jewelry. Depending on the outfit they are matched with, they can be everything from super glamorous to boho chic.

Finished Size
Length: approximately 2" (5cm)

Difficulty Level
Beginner

Techniques Used
Basic ISK Stitch and Base
Releasing from the Base
Decreasing Stitches
Using a drawplate

Tools
U.S. size 12, 14, or 10 (0.75, 0.6, or 1mm) crochet hook
Base of 12 stitches
Drawplate
Wire cutter
Flat-nose pliers

Materials
46' (14m) 28-gauge dead soft wire

Findings
Two 1½" (4cm) diameter wire hoops

Step 1

Leaving an 8″ (20 cm) tail, wire crochet 42 rows of ISK stitches on the 12 stitch base. [1]

Step 2

Release the knitting from the base.

Step 3

Insert the starting tail wire into the loop that is coming out to create a stitch. [2] Decrease stitches on the side released from the base until 4 stitches remain. [3]

Step 4

Place the four last loops one on top of the other and wrap them together twice. [4] Trim excess wire and tuck in the end.

Step 5

Pull the tube through the drawplate holes, starting with a hole of $^2/_3$″ (15mm) diameter. Pull the tube back out from the hole. Gradually go through decreasingly smaller holes until you have gone through the $^1/_3$″ (8 mm) diameter hole. [5]

Step 6

Measure the tube length to make sure it is 5″ (12.5cm). If the tube is too short, add a few rows and repeat Step 5. If it's too long, open up a few rows.

Step 7

Repeat Steps 3 and 4 at the other end of the crocheted tube. [6]

Step 8

String the crocheted tube onto the ear wire. [7-8]

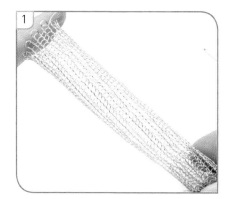

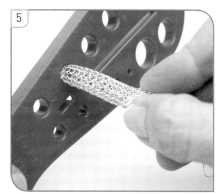

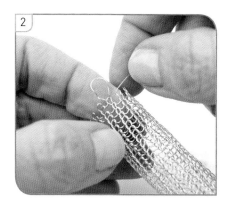

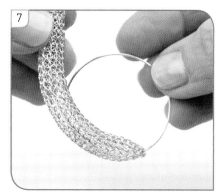

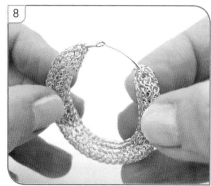

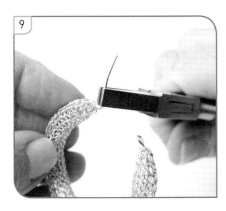

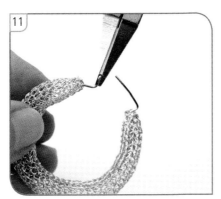

Step 9
Bend the straight side of the hoop 90°, [9] make a second bend approximately 1/16" (3mm) up from that point. [10]

Step 10
Straighten the ear wire edge with the flat-nose pliers. Twist the looped side of the ear wire 90°. [11-12]

Step 11
Repeat previous steps for the second earring.

Swirl Earrings

The Swirl Earrings are a chic statement accessory, great for a night out. They have volume and presence, while being very light to wear.

Finished Size
Length: approximately 2" (5cm)

Difficulty Level
Intermediate

Techniques Used
Basic ISK Stitch and Base
Releasing from the Base
Interweaving Beads & Stones
Flattening Designs
Flat Stitch
Decreasing Stitches

Tools
U.S. size 12, 14, or 10 (0.75, 0.6, or 1mm) crochet hook
Base of 8 stitches
Wire cutter
Flat-nose pliers
U.S. size 11 and 15 (8 and 10mm) knitting needles

Materials
13' (3.6mm) 28-gauge dead soft wire
Thirty 4mm pearls

Findings
Two ear wires
Two jump rings

Step 1

String 15 beads onto a 6 $\frac{1}{2}$' (1.9m) length of wire. [1]

Step 2

Leaving a tail of 4" (10 cm), wire crochet two rows using Basic ISK Stitch and a 8 stitch base.

Step 3

Starting with the third row, interweave one pearl between the first and second stitch. [2] Continue adding a bead every other row in the same space between the first and second stitch until all 15 pearls have been stitched. When complete 32 rows in total have been worked. To make the crocheted tube look even, insert a U.S. size 15 (10mm) knitting needle to stretch the tube. [3]

Step 4

Wire crochet an additional two more rows. Release the knitting from the base.

Step 5

Repeat Steps 1-4 for the second earring.

Step 6

Flatten the tube with the pearls running along one edge, Do not stretch the strap. [4]

Step 8

Close the end released from the base with flat stitches (see page 34). [5] Wrap the wires twice and cut them short.

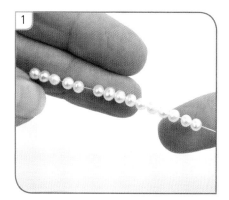

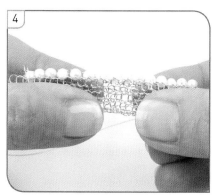

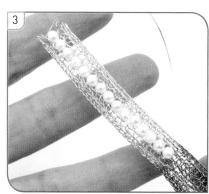

Step 9

Open the flatten end of tube still connected to the working wire. Decrease stitches around until 2 stitches remain. [6] Cut the wire leaving a 2 $^3/_4$" (7cm) tail.

Step 10

Wrap the wire around both loops to create a single wrapped loop.

Step 11

Repeat Steps 6-10 on the second earring component.

Step 12

One at a time, wrap each strap around a U.S. size 11 (8mm) knitting needle—alternatively, use a pen or something similar. [7-8]

Step 13

Using flat-nose pliers, connect the swirled straps to the jump ring on the ear wire. [9]

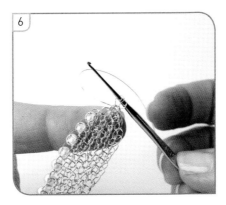

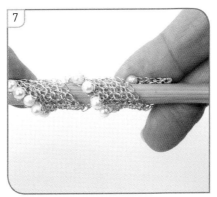

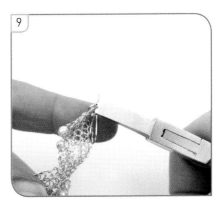

Nested Crystals with Pearl Earrings

These Nested Crystal with Pearl Earrings are small, sparkly, and elegant. The combination of wire work and crystal make for a magical effect.

Finished Size
Length: $^3/_4$" (1.8cm)
Width: $^1/_2$" (1cm)

Difficulty Level
Intermediate

Techniques Used
Basic ISK Stitch and Base
Releasing from the Base
Decreasing Stitches
Flattening Designs
Flat Stitch

Tools
U.S. size 12, 14, or 10 (0.75, 0.6, or 1mm)
crochet hook
Base of 12 stitches
Wire cutter
Flat-nose pliers

Materials
4 $^2/_3$' (1.4m) 28-gauge dead soft wire
Two 16mm Swarovski teardrop crystals
Two 4 mm pearls

Findings
Two ear wires

Step 1

Leaving a 12" (30cm) tail of wire wrapped into a coil, wire crochet two rows of ISK stitches on a 12 stitch base. [1]

Step 2

Make a row of decrease stitches. [2]

Step 3

Continue decreasing until 3 stitches remain. [3]

Step 4

Using the hook, place the three stitches one on top of the other in the center. [4]

Step 5

Release the work from the base. [5]

Step 6

Secure the three center stitches by wrapping them together twice, then cut the wire short.

Step 7

Flatten the disk-like element with your fingers and slightly stretch it. [6]

Step 8

Insert the tail you left at Step 1 into the loop from which it is coming out—this creates a new loop. [7]

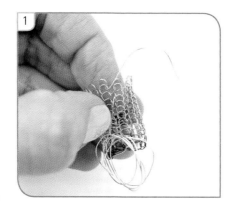

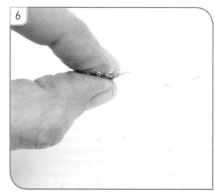

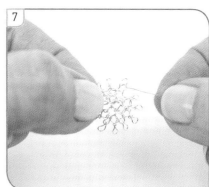

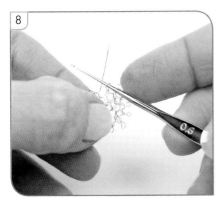

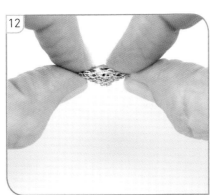

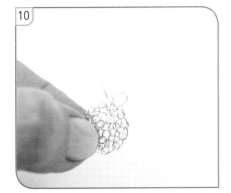

Step 9

Insert the hook into the loop to the right of this new stitch, [8] crochet around a flat stitch working to the right. [9] When you finish a whole circle go again into the first stitch so there's no gap left. Pull the wire out. [10]

Step 10

Place the crystal in the center of the wire disc [11] and mold the wires to surround it. [12] If it's too small, stretch the mesh element until it fits. [13]

Step 11

String a pearl onto the wire. Thread the wire through the hole from the front to the back. [14] Then string it back to the front through the crochet and again into the pearl, then into the back on the other side. [15]

Step 12

Secure the wire at the back and cut the wire short.

Step 13

Insert the hook at the back of the crochet behind two wires to create a loop the ear wire can hang on. [16] Twist these loops 90° to make them perpendicular to the work. [17]

Step 14

Attach the ear wire to the two loops. [18]

Step 15

Make a second identical earring.

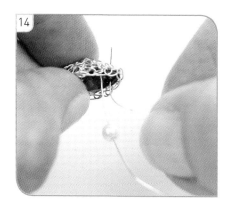

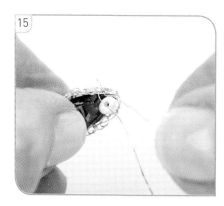

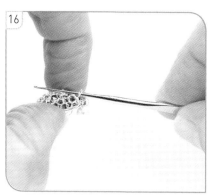

Shell Earrings

These Shell Earrings are large yet very light to wear. They look stunning teamed with short hair, and will add romantic flair to any outfit.

Finished Size
1.8in (4cm) long,
Width: ½" (1.5cm) wide

Difficulty Level
Intermediate

Techniques Used
Basic ISK Stitch and Base
Releasing from the Base
Decreasing Stitches
Flat Stitch

Tools
U.S. size 12, 14, or 10 (0.75, 0.6, or 1mm)
crochet hook
Base of 40 stitches
Wire cutter
Flat-nose pliers

Materials
7 ⅓' (2.2m) 28-gauge dead soft wire

Findings
Two ear wires

Step 1
Leaving a 23" (60cm) wire tail wrapped into a coil. [1]

Step 2
Work a row of decrease stitches. [2]

Step 3
Work a basic ISK stitch row. [3]

Step 4
Work a row of decrease stitches. Hold the work from beneath so the work can close towards becoming a dome shape. [4]

Step 5
Make two regular ISK stitch rows.

Step 6
Decrease stitches until three stitches remain. [5] Using the hook, place the three stitches one on top of the other in the center. [6]

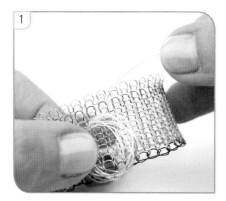

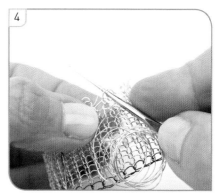

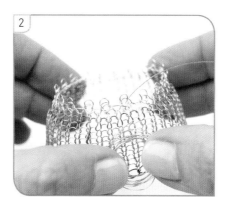

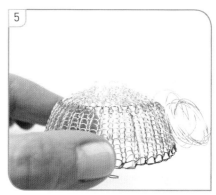

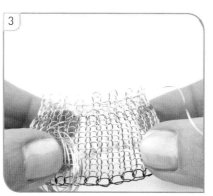

Step 7

Release the work from the base. [7]

Step 8

Secure the three center stitches by wrapping them together twice, [8] cut the wire short.

Step 9

Flatten the component with your fingers.

Step 10

Create a new stitch—using the tail from Step 1, pull the wire into the loop it is coming out from. [9]

Step 11

Fold the disk-like element leaving the new stitch and the one next to it untouched, they will later be wrapped together and function as the ear wire hangers. [10]

Step 12

Insert the hook into two stitches, one from both sides of the fold and pull a new stitch. [11] Work 6 flat stitches continuing to join the edges of the component. [12]

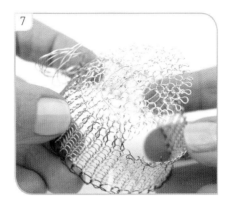

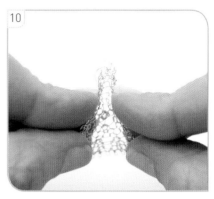

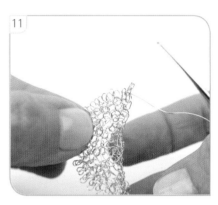

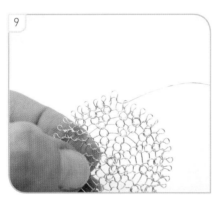

Step 13

Working around the outside edge and no longer joining the fold, continue in flat stitch around the component edge. [13]

Step14

Once you have reached the connected stitches from the other side, make one last stitch to close the gap.

Step 15

Thread the wire from the inner side of the shell to reach the first two loops. [14]

Note: These loops will connect to the ear wires and allow the component to dangle.

Step 16

Wrap the wire tight around both loops to bond them together. [15]

Step 17

Hang the shell on an ear wire using flat-nose pliers to secure the loop. [16-17]

Step 18

Make a second identical earring.

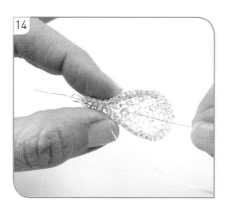

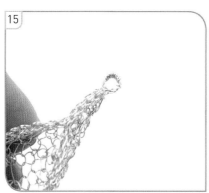

Dainty Pearl Ring

The Dainty Pearl Ring is a delicate piece of jewelry, especially appreciated by young people, and can be made with or without the pearl.

Finished Size
Width: ¼" (5mm)
Circumference: adjustable

Difficulty Level
Advanced

Techniques Used
Basic ISK Stitch
Making a Small Base
Releasing from the Base
Flattening Designs
Flat Stitch

Tools
U.S. size 12, 14, or 10 (0.75, 0.6, or 1mm) crochet hook
Base of 4 stitches
Wire cutter
Flat-nose pliers
U.S. size 1 (2.5mm) knitting needle

Materials
3' (91.4cm) 28-gauge dead soft wire
One 4mm pearl bead
Superglue/fast acting glue

Step 1

Note: *These instructions are for a ring size 7 (for other ring sizes see the chart on page 119).*

Leaving a $^3/_4$" (2cm) tail of wire, crochet 19 rows of ISK stitches on the 4 loop base. [1]

Step 2

Release the work from the base.

Step 3

Insert a U.S. size 1 (2.5mm) knitting needle into the tube to even out the work. [2]

Step 4

Flatten the tube. [3]

Step 5

Crochet together the two ends of the ring using flat stitch. Cut the wire and pull it through the last stitch. [4]

Step 6

Flatten the connected stitches using flat-nose pliers. [5]

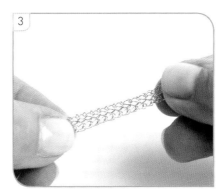

Step 7

String a bead onto one of the tails outside the ring, [6] then secure it to the ring by going through it twice. Cut the wire short. String the other tail through the bead as well, [7] cut it short. [8]

Step 8

Gently drop liquid superglue into the bead hole to keep the bead from spinning when worn. [9]

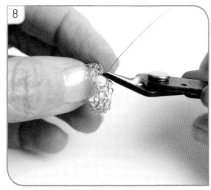

Ring Size Chart

Other ring sizes are created by making more or fewer rows at Step 1.

The exact size greatly depends on the tension of your work. If your work is tight you might need to make more rows than suggested, if your work is loose you should make fewer. This size chart is for average tension.

Ring size	Number of rows
5	17
6	18
7	19
8	20
9	21
10	22
11	23
12	24

Wide Beaded Ring

This Wide Beaded Ring can be as individual as you are; here the crocheted mesh functions as your canvas, so use your creativity!

Finish Size
Width: ¾" (1.8cm) wide
Circumference: adjustable

Difficulty Level
Intermediate

Techniques Used
Basic ISK Stitch and Base
Releasing from the Base
Interweaving Beads and Stones
Flattening Designs
Flat Stitch

Tools
U.S. size 12, 14, or 10 (0.75, 0.6, or 1mm)
crochet hook
Base of 10 stitches
Wire cutter
Flat-nose pliers

Materials
15' (4.6m) 28-gauge dead soft wire
Twenty-five 2mm faceted beads

Step 1

String the beads onto the wire. The following instructions show two variations.

Option1: Beads all the same color. String 25 beads.

Option 2: One line of accent color down the center. String the beads in the following order [1]:
11 in color #1
3 in color #2
11 in color #1

Step 2

Note: These instructions are for a ring size 7 (for other ring sizes see the chart on page 123).

Leaving a 1" (2.5cm) wire tail, wire crochet seven rows of ISK stitches on a 10 stitch base. [2]

Step 3

On rows 8–12 (a total of 5 rows) insert beads between every two stitches only between stitches 5–10, five beads on each row. This will place all the beads on the outer side of the ring. [3]

Step 4

Continue crocheting another seven rows of regular ISK stitches. [4]

Step 5

Release the work from the base. [5]

Step 6

Flatten the tube with the beads all on one face of the strap. [6] Stretch the strap to make it longer and softer. If required, align the beads using the crochet hook by pressing it into the spaces between the beads. [7]

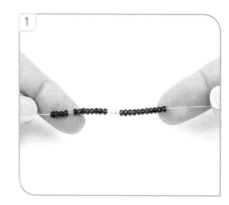

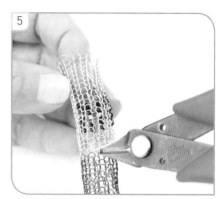

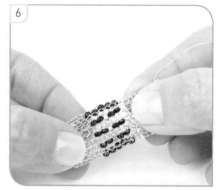

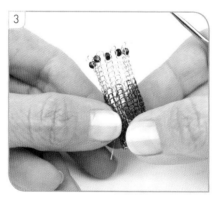

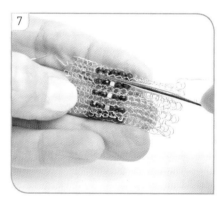

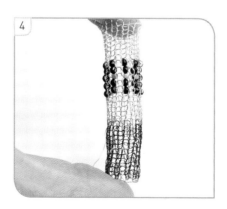

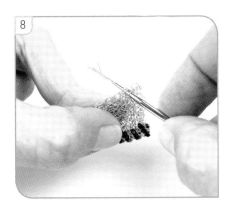

Step 7
Crochet together the two ends of the ring using a flat stitch. [8] Pull the wire through the last stitch.

Step 8
Flatten the connecting area using flat-nose pliers. [9]

Step 9
Secure the two tails ends and cut the wire short. [10]

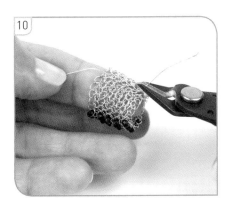

Ring Size Chart
For a larger or smaller ring with the contrasting center bead pattern, use the following combinations.

Ring Number size	Bead pattern	of rows
5	6 + 5 + 6	17
6	7 + 5 + 6	18
7	7 + 5 + 7	19
8	8 + 5 + 7	20
9	8 + 5 + 8	21
10	9 + 5 + 8	22
11	9 + 5 + 9	23

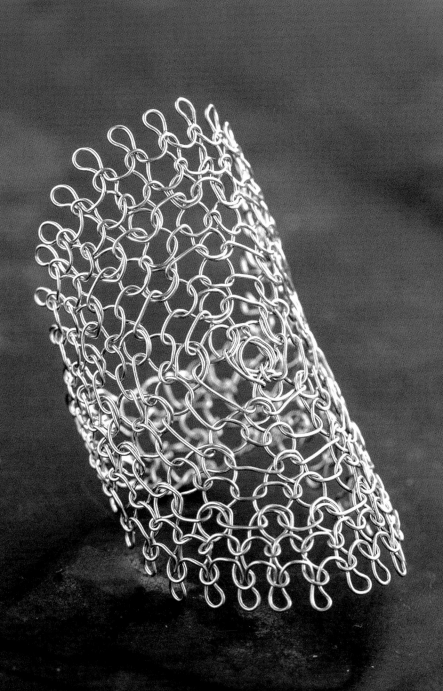

Full Finger Tattoo Ring

The full finger tattoo ring is a combination of the romantic feel of a lace and the more edgy one of a tattoo; it's a delicate piece of jewelry, with unique statement presence.

Finished Size
Center motif: 1½" (4cm) diameter
Ring Circumference: adjustable

Difficulty Level
Intermediate

Techniques Used
Basic ISK Stitch and Base
Releasing from the Base
Decreasing Stitches
Changing Wires
One-layer Mesh
Flat Stitch

Tools
U.S. size 12, 14, or 10 (0.75, 0.6, or 1mm)
crochet hook
Base of 40 stitches
Wire cutter
Flat-nose pliers

Materials:
7 ¹/₃' (2.2m) 28-gauge dead soft wire

Step 1
Leaving a 4" (10 cm) tail of wire, wire crochet three rows of Basic ISK Stitch using a 40 stitch base. [1]

Step 2
Work a row of decrease stitches—20 stitches remain. [2]

Step 3
Work a row of ISK stitches.

Step 4
Work a row of decrease stitches—10 stitches remain. [3]

Note: *From this point start holding the work from beneath while you close the dome.*

Step 5
Make a regular row of stitches.

Step 6
Decrease pairs of stitches until you are three stitches remain. Using the hook, place them one on top of the other in the center. [4]

Step 7
Release the work from the base. [5]

Step 8
Secure the center of the flower by wrapping the three stitches together twice, and then cut the wire short. [6]

Step 9
Flatten the flower with your fingers, you can also hammer it gently. [7]

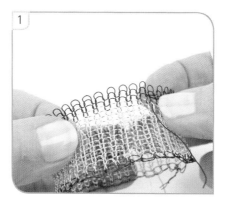

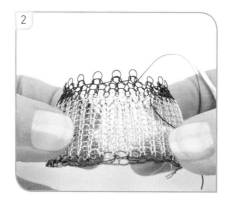
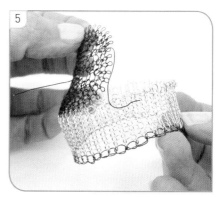
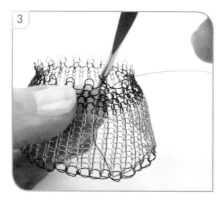
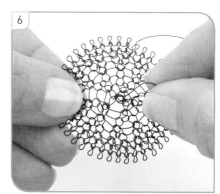
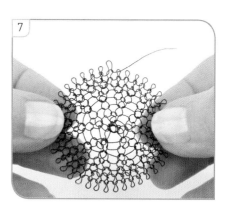

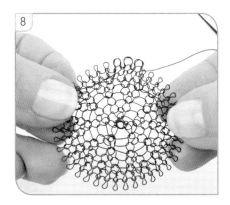

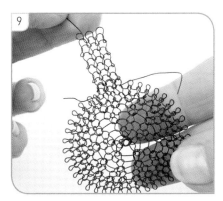

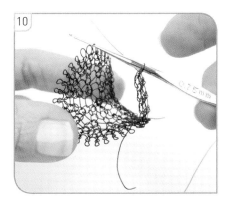

Step 10

Form a loop by inserting the tail from Step 1 into the loop it is coming out from. Change to a new wire. Crochet this same stitch with the new wire as well, make an additional two stitches using both wires. [8]

Step 11

For a ring size 9, work nine rows of one-layer mesh. [9] For a larger ring, work additional rows; for a smaller ring size, work fewer rows.

Step 12

Connect the end of the one-layer crochet mesh to the three stitches on the opposite side of the tattoo flower working flat stitches. [10]

Step 13

Use chain-nose pliers to flatten the joint just made. [11] Wrap each of the three tails twice, and cut them short.

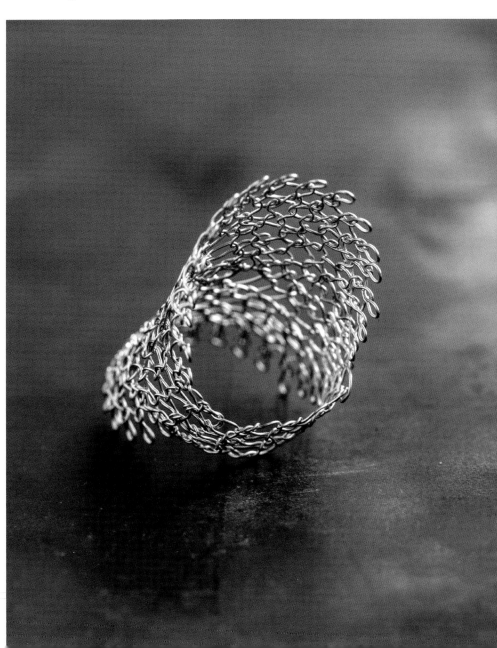

Acknowledgements

I would like to thank my dear family, Avner, Hagar, and Nimrod, for supporting me all along the bumpy road. First by encouraging me to take my hobby seriously until it turned into my day job, and then for being so patient during the process of writing this book.

I also want like to thank all my teachers along the years, starting with my grandma who taught me how to crochet in the first place.

Then there's Claudia Segal, who edited my first e-book many years ago and might not remember, but was the first person that suggested I publish a printed book. Needless say, at the time it sounded impossible.

With more present thanks, I would like to thank Jo Bryant for initiating this project, believing in it, and in me, and for making it happen.

Less specific yet just as important, are the thanks to all my loyal customers that have been buying my e-books and tools for more than a decade now, and through this also supporting my ISK community to grow beyond boundaries, I wish I could name and thank you all individually.

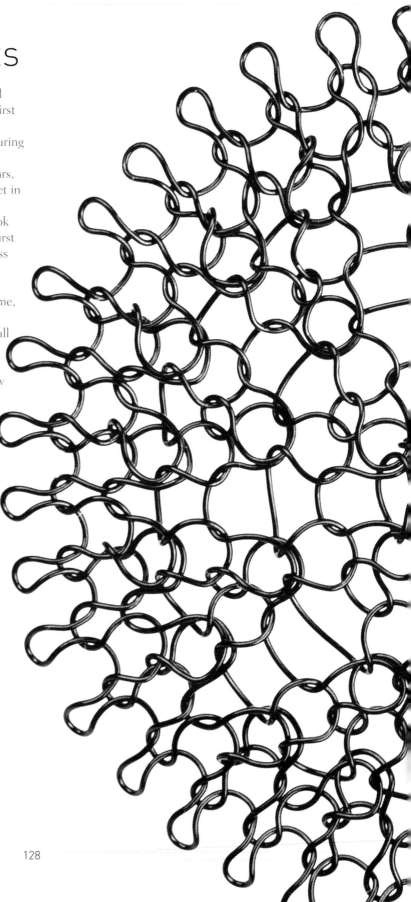